THE POWER TO REJOICE

21 Days to Victory over Your Problems

Vernon L. Williams, M.S.

Author of *Paddle Your Own Boat: 10 Rules that Guarantee Career Success*

Library of Congress Cataloging-in-Publication Data
Williams, Vernon

The Power to Rejoice: 21 Days to Victory Over Your Problems/
Vernon Williams

Includes bibliographical references and index.
ISBN 0-9777338-8-2

Published by Empowerment Publishers.

This book is available at quantity discounts with bulk purchase. For more information, please call 866-850-3354.

Contents

Introduction

I want to rejoice but I am struggling with:

- Work/Career Problems
- Physical Health Problems
- Emotional Health Problems
- Death of a loved one
- Financial Problems
- Family Problems

Does this sound like you or someone you love? If not, it probably will in the future. As Jesus said, "In this world you will have trouble." (John 16:33a)

Yet, the Apostle Paul tells us to "Rejoice in the Lord always. I will say it again: Rejoice!" (Philippians 4:4) When he commands us to "Rejoice" and repeats it, it is comparable to a flashing red light saying **"This is critical"**, **"Don't miss it!"**

Despite this critical command, instead of rejoicing, we become downcast when we experience problems.

Imagine yourself rejoicing, even as you are experiencing one (or more) of the problems listed above.

The purpose of this book is to show you how to make that image a reality.

I am sure you have several questions:

1. What qualifies me to write this book?

I have studied human behavior and motivation for more than thirty years. I have a master's degree in Applied Behavior Science from Johns Hopkins University. I completed a year-long church leadership program, which included Bible study methods and counseling. Brent T. Brooks, Th.M, former adjunct faculty member of Capital Bible Seminary and founding pastor of Grace Community Church, mentored me for three years. I have more than twenty-five years of counseling experience.

I have experienced problems. I was passed over for promotion. I was laid off from my job two years before retirement.

I was my wife's caregiver for 12 years. After 34 years of marriage, she went to be with the Lord. I have had business setbacks, dealt with financial challenges and relational conflicts. One brother was killed in combat, another died of a heart attack at age 37, still another brother committed suicide, just to name a few of the problems I have faced. Through it all, I have rejoiced.

2. How could I rejoice during such problems?

    a. I used the strategy that I present in this book.

    b. I accepted the Apostle Paul's invitation to imitate him. "Follow my example, as I follow the example of Christ." (1 Corinthians 11:1)

3. What problems did Paul encounter?

His fellow Jews plotted to kill him, he was stoned and left for dead, he was persecuted and expelled, he spent two years in prison, he was shipwrecked, he was beaten, and at times he was hungry, thirsty and naked. Finally, he had a thorn in the flesh.

4. What was Paul's reaction to his problems?

He rejoiced. "Not only so, but we also rejoice in our sufferings, because we know that suffering produces perseverance; perseverance, character; and character, hope." (Romans 5:3-4)

Allow me to make a key point:

Paul said he rejoiced. He did not say he was happy. I believe there is a difference between the two.

Happiness is an emotion based on circumstances. For that reason, it can be like a roller coaster ride. We are happy if we get promoted and receive a nice pay raise. We are unhappy if we get laid off or are forced to take a pay cut. We are happy if we are healthy. We are unhappy if we are diagnosed with cancer. We are happy if we have all of our children present. We are unhappy if one of them dies. We are happy if we are in a healthy relationship. We are unhappy if the relationship ends.

Joy, on the other hand, is a state of mind. It is not based on circumstances. Instead, it is an **approach to life** rather than a **reaction to life**. It is the lens through which we see events.

We can rejoice in the midst of problems. So, while I was not happy when I was laid off two years before retirement, I rejoiced.

5. What did Paul do that enabled him to rejoice during his problems?

a. Paul did not "Rejoice in his circumstances" or "Rejoice in himself." He "Rejoiced in the Lord." Why? Because Jesus Christ, who is the same yesterday, today and forever, was the source of his joy. When Paul rejoiced in the Lord, his attention was focused on Him; who He is and who Paul is in Him.

b. He focused on John 16:33b "But take heart! I have overcome the world." (In John 16a Jesus says: "In this world you will have trouble.")

c. He looked to the future. "I consider that our present sufferings are not worth comparing with the glory that will be revealed in us." (Romans 8:18)

    d. He recognized that God was using his problems to make him more like Jesus.

"And we know that in all things God works for the good of those who love him, who have been called according to his purpose. For those God foreknew, he also predestined to be conformed to the likeness of his Son, that he might be the firstborn among many brothers." (Romans 8:28-29)

    e. He recognized that his problems were temporary.

"For our light and momentary troubles are achieving for us an eternal glory that far outweighs them all. So we fix our eyes not on what is seen, but on what is unseen. For what is seen is temporary, but what is unseen is eternal." (2 Corinthians 4:17-18)

    f. He recognized that his problems enabled him to tap into God's power.

But he said to me, "My grace is sufficient for you, for my power is made perfect in weakness." Therefore, I will boast all the more gladly about my weaknesses, so that Christ's power may rest on me." (2 Corinthians 12:9)

    g. He believed that God would meet all of his needs as he was going through his problems.

"My God will meet all your needs according to his glorious riches in Christ Jesus." (Philippians 4:19)

    h. He viewed dying as a good thing.

"For to me, to live is Christ and to die is gain." (Philippians 1:21)

6. How could Paul sustain such a positive perspective in the midst of so many problems?

He managed his thought life (self-talk*).

a. He recognized that he had a choice; he could think negative thoughts (God is punishing me for my role in persecuting, torturing and killing Christians before I became a Christian) or he could think positive thoughts (I have gained forgiveness and I have a new calling since becoming a Christian).

b. He recognized that Satan would send negative thoughts his way. "Put on the whole armor of God, that you may be able to stand against the devil's scheming." (Ephesians 6:11)

c. He recognized that his thoughts determined how he felt. If he thought negative thoughts he would feel downcast; if he thought positive thoughts he would rejoice.

d. He chose positive thoughts and focused on his new calling. "Forgetting those things which are behind and reaching forward to those things which are ahead." (Philippians 3:13)

e. He thought about God's truth rather than Satan's lies. "Whatever is true, whatever is noble, whatever is right, whatever is pure, whatever is lovely, whatever is admirable-if anything is excellent or praiseworthy-think about such things." (Philippians 4:8)

*The term "self-talk" has become popular in recent decades. Psychologists say that we *verbalize* much--if not most--of our thinking. Let me give you an example. Suppose you wake up in the morning and the radio announcer says it is raining. You do not just have a vague sense of disappointment. You would actually verbalize negative messages to yourself, such as, "Traffic is going to be backed up", "I am probably not going to get a good parking space", and "I am going to be late for my meeting." When we consider what goes on in our minds, we realize that we are constantly speaking constructively or destructively to ourselves.

These endless messages that we verbalize to ourselves determine our feeling (joy or gloom). The joy or gloom determines the actions we take. The actions we take determine whether we achieve our goals. Here's how it works: If you tell yourself "I am never going to get a job," you will feel discouraged, put forth a half-hearted effort and not get a job. On the other hand, if you tell yourself, "I know I will get a job that matches my skills", you will feel encouraged, put forth a relentless effort, and ultimately find that job.

The Bible, by the way, has lots of examples of "Self-Talk". In Psalm 42:11, the psalmist asks himself, "Why are you downcast, O my soul? Why so disturbed within me?" He commanded himself to "Put your hope in God." Another example of self-talk appears in Genesis 17:17, "Abraham fell on his face and laughed, and said in his heart, "Will a son be born to a man a hundred years old? And Sarah, who is ninety years old, bear a child?"

The great news is that, with concentrated and sustained effort, we can change our negative self-talk to positive self-talk, thereby experiencing joy.

7. How did Paul change his negative self-talk to positive self-talk?

He took captive every thought to make sure it was obedient to Christ. (2 Corinthians 10:5)

Having taken hold of every thought, he either affirmed it to be **true**, **noble**, **right**, **pure**, **lovely**, **admirable**, **excellent** or **praiseworthy**, (Philippians 4:8) or he replaced it with a scriptural truth.

8. Do you have a system to help me change my negative self-talk to positive self-talk?

Yes. I have identified 26 problems that come our way most frequently. For each problem, I have included nine steps to help you change your negative self-talk to positive self-talk.

9. Can I easily incorporate the system into my life?

Yes. The central step of the system requires you to devote 15 minutes per day for 21 days to meditating on selected verses from God's word that are related to the problem you are facing.

10. How can I get the most out of this book?

a. Turn to the Contents page.
b. Find the problem you are facing.
c. Go to the chapter that provides the prescription for victory over that problem.
d. Follow the 9 steps presented.
e. Use the "Living a Joyful Life" discussion with your small group.

Finally, even though it will be challenging, the Scripture suggests that we can change our self-talk. "After the Lord your God has driven them out before you, do not say to yourself. "The Lord has brought me here to take possession of this land because of my righteousness. No, it is on account of the wickedness of these nations that the Lord is going to drive them out before you." (Deuteronomy 9:4)

The fact that God tells us what not to say to ourselves suggests that we have to power to control what we tell ourselves.

Start rejoicing today. God bless you.

November 20, 2012
Columbia, Maryland

Note: Scripture verses are taken from the New International Version and the New King James Version of the Bible.

Part one

WORK/CAREER PROBLEMS

Chapter One

I Lost My Job

ALTHOUGH LAYOFFS ARE common today, losing your job cannot steal your joy. What you choose to say to yourself about losing your job can. Why? What you choose to say to yourself determines how you feel. For example, if you tell yourself, "I will never get another job" you will feel discouraged. On the other hand, if you tell yourself, "I know I will find a job soon" you will be able to rejoice.

You cannot control whether you lose your job. You can control what you say to yourself about losing your job. In order to rejoice, you must replace the negative statements/questions that you say to yourself. These nine steps will help you accomplish that:

1. **Examine typical negative statements/questions that people say to themselves:**

   "I am angry with my company for laying me off."
   "How am I going to pay my bills?"
   "I am never going to find another job."
   "I can't get a job because the economy is bad."
   "I have not gone on a job interview in over 20 years."

2. List negative statements/questions that you say to yourself in the left column below:

Negative statements/ questions	Replace each with a verse from today's passage in Step 3

3. Meditate*on today's passage for 15 minutes per day for the next 21 days.

"Fix these words of mine in your hearts and minds; tie them as symbols on your hands and bind them on your foreheads. Teach them to your children, talking about them when you sit at home and when you walk along the road, when you lie down and when you get up." (Deuteronomy 11:18-19)

Day	Today's Passage
1	Matthew 6:31-32
2	Psalm 23:1
3	Luke12:24
4	Philippians 4:19
5	Psalm 37:25
6	Psalm 37:8
7	Philippians 3:13-14
8	Romans 8:28
9	Lamentations 3:22-23
10	John 15:5
11	Psalm 127:1
12	John 14:14
13	Isaiah 40:31
14	Psalm 33:20
15	Deuteronomy 31:6
16	Hebrews 10:23
17	Psalm 34:19
18	Psalm 42:11
19	2 Corinthians 4:17-18
20	1 Peter 5:7
21	1 Thessalonians 5:17

*When I say "meditate" I do not mean incantations or lotus postures. Instead, I mean a time where you block out busy routines – prayer lists, study requirements, etc.

   a. Read the verse out loud two times.
   b. What does the verse mean to you now that you have lost your job?
   c. Do you believe the verse with your mind and your heart?
   d. How will you think differently?
   e. How will I act differently?

f. Memorize the verse.

Everyone wants to rejoice. But that can seem like mission impossible after you have lost your job. However, meditating on the verses in Step 3 for 15 minutes per day for 21 days will give you victory over your negative statements/questions. Then, you will be able to rejoice in the Lord.

4. Replace each negative statement/question you listed in Step 2 with a verse from today's passage in Step 3.

For example, replace: "I have not gone on a job interview in 20 years."

With: "I can do everything through Him who gives me strength." (Philippians 4:13)

5. Keep a journal.

The Lord gave me this answer, "Write down clearly what I reveal to you." (Habakkuk 2:2)

Some things you might want to record in your journal:

   a. Your thoughts
   b. Prayers
   c. Answers you have seen to prayers
   d. Things you have learned
   e. Progress (or lack thereof) you have made

6. Select an accountability partner.

"Two are better than one, because they have a good reward for their labor. For if they fall, one will lift up his companion. But woe to him who is alone when he falls, for he has no one to help him up." (Ecclesiastes 4:9)

a. An accountability partner

1) Helps clarify goals. Sharing your goals with someone moves you towards achieving them.

2) Offers encouragement. A partner encourages you to keep moving towards your goals.

3) Challenges you. There may be times when you need a little "tough love". A partner reminds you of what you are working towards and how it will change your life.

b. What to look for when selecting an accountability partner

1) Trust. Select someone that you trust. Otherwise, you will never get the full benefits of the relationship.

2) Honesty. Select someone who will be completely honest with you.

3) Confidentiality. Select someone who will keep all information discussed between the two of you, without any exceptions.

4) Non-judgmental. Select someone who understands that their role is to listen, ask questions and offer feedback, but never to judge.

5) Common Core Beliefs. Select someone who shares your beliefs. For example, if you believe it is possible to control your feelings by controlling your thinking, your accountability partner should believe the same thing.

c. How to get the maximum benefit from an accountability partner

1) Be clear on your goal(s).

2) Meet with your partner (face-to-face or by telephone) once per week for three weeks.

3) Make notes in your journal on progress so you can follow-up at the next meeting.

4) Keep the commitment to meet on the agreed-upon date at the agreed-upon time.

7. Draw inspiration from a man who chose to rejoice despite losing his job.

Joel relates this story:

My family and I were living a comfortable, middle class lifestyle. I was working at an automobile manufacturer and my wife was a stay-at-home mom for our two kids. Suddenly, I was laid off from my job. I was angry at my employer. After three months of searching, the only job I could find was in retail sales. Although I was grateful for a job, the pay was not nearly what I had been making in the auto industry. Of course, the bills continued as they had been when I was making a larger salary. I was sure there was no way we could manage.

There were times when we were getting down to the last bit of food. However, at just that time, one of the neighbors would bring over some food, or another neighbor would invite us over for dinner and give us lots of leftovers to take home with us. Praise God!

My wife and I prayed and meditated on Psalm 37:25: "I have been young, and now am old. Yet I have not seen the righteous forsaken, nor their descendants begging for bread." The more I read and prayed, the more peace I felt. My anger at my employer disappeared.

I found myself singing an old hymn, "Great is Thy Faithfulness"

I learned that the writer of the song, Thomas Chisholm, had accepted Christ as his Savior at age 27. Chisholm had been a magazine editor who was subsequently ordained a Methodist minister. However, due to failing health, he only did pastoral work for one year. Although his income was practically nonexistent, God continually met all of his needs. This inspired him to write *Great is Thy Faithfulness*.

"Great is Thy faithfulness!

Great is Thy faithfulness!

Morning by morning new mercies I see;

All I have needed Thy hand hath provided – Great is Thy faithfulness, Lord, unto me!"

As time went on, I struggled to make my car payments. Although I was not sure how God was going to work it out, having seen what He had done in the past, I rejoiced in the knowledge that He would.

Sure enough, just as my wife and I were discussing the car situation, my supervisor discovered that I qualified for a newly created position. My pay increased enough for me to maintain my car. Praise God!

It took almost two years, but I was reinstated to my former job with the automobile manufacturer. The good news does not end there. When I was reinstated, I received two years of back pay. Praise God, indeed!

Summary: Joel started out being angry and doubtful. He ended up rejoicing and praising God. In between, he changed his thoughts from his circumstances to God's promises.

In addition to rejoicing, Stephen Gallison used losing his job as an opportunity to serve others. While laid off, he wrote a proposal for a federal grant to provide free outplacement services to professionals, executives, managers, and to technical and scientific employees. The grant was awarded and Stephen became the founding director of The Professional Outplacement Assistance Center (POAC). The program operates under the Maryland Department of Labor, Licensing and Regulation. It has been designated as a "Best Practices" program and was recently named an "Innovative Design" program by the U.S Department of Labor. The program has served more than 205,000 Maryland residents since its creation.

8. Draw inspiration from how God brought you through a previous problem.

"Remember how the LORD your God led you all the way in the wilderness these forty years, to humble and test you in order to know what was in your heart, whether or not you would keep his commands. He humbled you, causing you to hunger and then feeding you with manna, which neither you nor your ancestors had known, to teach you that man does not live on bread alone but on every word that comes from the mouth of the LORD. Your clothes did not wear out and your feet did not swell during these forty years." (Deuteronomy 8:2-4)

   a. List a problem that you had in the past.

   b. Describe how God brought you through it.

9. Guard against negative statements/questions.

"We demolish arguments and every pretension that sets itself up against the knowledge of God, and we take captive every thought to make it obedient to Christ." (2 Corinthians 10:5)

Since you have grown accustomed to making negative statements/questions to yourself about losing your job, you will be inclined to continue doing so. When you are tempted, ask yourself, "Is this statement/question aligned with what God says?" If not, immediately replace it with a verse from today's passage in Step 3.

Chapter Two

I Don't Like My Job

MANY OF US HAVE HAD job we did not like. It may have been due to low pay, gossiping colleagues, unhappy customers, boring work, a difficult boss or some other reason. However, being in a job you don't like cannot steal your joy. What you choose to say to yourself about being in a job you don't like can. Why? What you say to yourself determines how you feel. For example, if you tell yourself, "I hate my job" you will feel down. On the other hand, if you tell yourself, "There are some things I like about my job" you will be able to rejoice.

You cannot control low pay, gossiping colleagues, unhappy customers, boring work and a difficult boss. You can control what you say to yourself. In order to rejoice, you must replace the negative statements/questions that you say to yourself. These nine steps will help you accomplish that:

1. **Examine typical negative statements/questions that people say to themselves:**

    "I hate my job."
    "I will do the absolute minimum that I can get away with."
    "Even though I have been looking for another job this has dragged on for 5 years."
    "I am very uncomfortable in this situation."
    "Although I have not taken any action, I have faith God is going to get me another job."

2. **List negative statements/questions that you say to yourself in the left column below:**

Negative statements/ questions	Replace each with a verse from today's passage in Step 3

3. **Meditate on today's passage for 15 minutes per day for the next 21 days.**

"Fix these words of mine in your hearts and minds; tie them as symbols on your hands and bind them on your foreheads. Teach them to your children, talking about them when you sit at home and when you walk along the road, when you lie down and when you get up." (Deuteronomy 11:18-19)

Day	Today's Passage
1	1 Thessalonians 5:18
2	Psalm 118:24
3	James 1:2-3
4	James 2:17
5	2 Corinthians 4:17-18
6	Colossians 3:23-24
7	Isaiah 40:31
8	Philippians 4:11
9	Ecclesiastes 9:10
10	Ecclesiastes 3:22
11	Proverbs 14:23
12	Proverbs 18:9
13	Proverbs 10:4
14	Proverbs 12:24
15	John 6:27
16	1 Corinthians 15:58
17	1 Corinthians 10:31
18	Colossians 3:17
19	Matthew 5:16
20	1 Peter 2:12
21	1 Thessalonians 5:17

*When I say "meditate" I do not mean incantations or lotus postures. Instead, I mean a time where you block out busy routines – prayer lists, study requirements, etc.

    a. Read the verse out loud two times.
    b. What does the verse mean to you now that you don't like your job?
    c. Do you believe the verse with your mind and your heart?
    d. How will you think differently?
    e. How will you act differently?

    f. Memorize the verse.

Everyone wants to rejoice. But that can seem like mission impossible when you have a job you don't like. However, meditating on the verses in Step 3 for 15 minutes per day for 21 days will give you victory over your negative statements/questions. Then, you will be able to rejoice in the Lord.

4. Replace each negative statement/question you listed in Step 2 with a verse from today's passage in Step 3.

For example, replace: "I hate my job."

With: "In everything, give thanks." (1 Thessalonians 5:18)

5. Keep a journal.

The Lord gave me this answer, "Write down clearly what I reveal to you." (Habakkuk 2:2)

Some things you might want to record in your journal:

    a. Your thoughts
    b. Prayers
    c. Answers you have seen to prayers
    d. Things you have learned
    e. Progress (or lack thereof) you have made

6. Select an accountability partner.

"Two are better than one, because they have a good reward for their labor. For if they fall, one will lift up his companion. But woe to him who is alone when he falls, for he has no one to help him up." (Ecclesiastes 4:9)

a. An accountability partner

1) Helps clarify goals. Sharing your goals with someone moves you towards achieving them.

2) Offers encouragement. A partner encourages you to keep moving towards your goals.

3) Challenges you. There may be times when you need a little "tough love". A partner reminds you of what you are working towards and how it will change your life.

b. What to look for when selecting an accountability partner

1) Trust. Select someone that you trust. Otherwise, you will never get the full benefits of the relationship.

2) Honesty. Select someone who will be completely honest with you.

3) Confidentiality. Select someone who will keep all information discussed between the two of you, without any exceptions.

4) Non-judgmental. Select someone who understands that their role is to listen, ask questions and offer feedback, but never to judge.

5) Common Core Beliefs. Select someone who shares your beliefs. For example, if you believe it is possible to control your feelings by controlling your thinking, your accountability partner should believe the same thing.

c. How to get the maximum benefit from an accountability partner

1) Be clear on your goal(s).

2) Meet with your partner (face-to-face or by telephone) once per week for three weeks.

3) Make notes in your journal on progress so you can follow-up at the next meeting.

4) Keep the commitment to meet on the agreed-upon date at the agreed-upon time.

7. Draw inspiration from a man who chose to rejoice despite not liking his job.

When Larry graduated from college with a terrific grade point average, he was very optimistic that he would find a job that matched his skills.

However, the only position he could find was in manufacturing. Needing to earn a living and with no other prospects, Larry accepted the position.

He was bored and unhappy immediately. His duties were repetitive and Larry considered himself overqualified for the position. He complained loudly to everyone who would listen about how the job was beneath him.

After several months of making himself and everyone around him miserable, Larry decided to turn to the Bible to see what God had to say. Two verses stood out immediately:

"I have learned in whatever state I am in to be content." (Philippians 4:11)

"In everything give thanks." (1 Thessalonians 5:18)

Larry set out to make himself content in his job.

In talking with some of his classmates, he found out that many of them were still searching for a job. So, he began thanking God that he had a job.

He read the story of Joseph, who was sold into slavery by his brothers. No matter what situation Joseph found himself in, he worked hard and remained faithful. As a result, he rose to the number two position just below the Pharaoh. From that position, God used Joseph to save his family and all of Egypt during a famine.

Larry also read Matthew 28:19: "Go and make disciples of all nations, baptizing them in the name of the Father and of the Son and of the Holy Spirit."

He began to think of his job as a mission field to which God had called him. He started quoting Scripture in conversations with his coworkers. His coworkers noticed the change in Larry. A group of them approached him a few months later and asked if he would consider leading a Bible study during lunch time. After praying, Larry agreed. Not long after beginning the bible study, one of his coworkers accepted Christ as her savior.

Having decided to remain in the job that he hated, Larry has found satisfaction and contentment in allowing God to use him to serve others right where he is.

Summary: Larry went from saying the job was beneath him, to rejoicing and thanking God for the opportunity to serve Him. He did so because he negated Satan's influence by allowing God's word to change what he said he said to himself.

8. Draw inspiration from how God brought you through a previous problem.

"Remember how the LORD your God led you all the way in the wilderness these forty years, to humble and test you in order to know what was in your heart, whether or not you would keep his commands. He humbled you, causing you to hunger and then feeding you with manna, which neither you nor your ancestors had known, to teach you that man does not live on bread alone but on every word that comes from the mouth of the LORD. Your clothes did not wear out and your feet did not swell during these forty years." (Deuteronomy 8:2-4)

a) List a problem you had in the past.

b) Describe how God brought you through it.

9. Guard against negative statements/questions.

"We demolish arguments and every pretension that sets itself up against the knowledge of God, and we take captive every thought to make it obedient to Christ." (2 Corinthians 10:5)

Since you have grown accustomed to making negative statements/questions to yourself about not liking your job, you will be inclined to continue doing so. When you are tempted, ask yourself, "Is this statement/question aligned with what God says?" If not, immediately replace it with a verse from today's passage in Step 3.

Chapter Three

I Have a Difficult Boss

DIFFICULT BOSSES can be challenging. However, having a difficult boss cannot steal your joy. What you choose to say to yourself about having a difficult boss can. Why? What you choose to say to yourself determines how you feel. For example, if you tell yourself, "I hate my boss" you will feel down. On the other hand, if you tell yourself, "I can learn some things from my boss" you will be able to rejoice.

You cannot control your boss' management style. You can control what you say to yourself. In order to rejoice, you must replace the negative statements/questions that you say to yourself. These nine steps will help you accomplish that:

1. **Examine typical negative statements/questions that people say to themselves:**

   "Even though my boss is incompetent, he has authority over me."
   "I tell my co-workers, friends, neighbors and church members what a difficult boss I have."
   "I am afraid to talk with my boss."
   "I get a knot in my stomach on Sunday night because I dread going to work on Monday."
   "My productivity has suffered as a result of my having such a difficult boss."

2. **List negative statements/questions that you say to yourself in the left column below:**

Negative statements/ questions	Replace each with a verse from today's passage in Step 3

3. **Meditate on today's passage for 15 minutes per day for the next 21 days.**

"Fix these words of mine in your hearts and minds; tie them as symbols on your hands and bind them on your foreheads. Teach them to your children, talking about them when you sit at home and when you walk along the road, when you lie down and when you get up." (Deuteronomy 11:18-19)

Day	Today's Passage
1	Romans 13:1
2	Ephesians 6:5-8
3	Matthew 18:15
4	Deuteronomy 31:6
5	Hebrews 13:6
6	Colossians 3:23-24
7	1 Peter 2:18
8	Psalm 118:24
9	Proverbs 17:22
10	Psalm 34:19
11	2 Corinthians 4:17-18
12	Colossians 3:13
13	Matthew 5:44-45
14	1 Corinthians 4:12
15	1 Peter 4:12-13
16	1 Peter 2:21-23
17	Philippians 2:14-16
18	2 Corinthians 5:20
19	1 Thessalonians 5:17
20	1 Thessalonians 5:18
21	2 Peter 1:5-7

*When I say "meditate" I do not mean incantations or lotus postures. Instead, I mean a time where you block out busy routines – prayer lists, study requirements, etc.

    a. Read the verse out loud two times.
    b. What does the verse mean to you now that you have a difficult boss?
    c. Do you believe the verse with your mind and your heart?
    d. How will you think differently?

   e. How will you act differently?
   f. Memorize the verse.

Everyone wants to rejoice. But that can seem like mission impossible when you have a difficult boss. However, meditating on the verses in Step 3 for 15 minutes per day for 21 days will give you victory over your negative statements/questions. Then, you will be able to rejoice in the Lord.

4. Replace each negative statement/question you listed in Step 2 with a verse from today's passage in Step 3.

For example, replace: "My productivity has gone down due to having such a difficult boss."

With: "Whatever you do, do it heartily, as to the Lord and not to men, knowing that from the Lord you will receive the reward of the inheritance; for you serve the Lord Christ." (Colossians 3:23-24)

5. Keep a journal.

The Lord gave me this answer, "Write down clearly what I reveal to you." (Habakkuk 2:2)

Some things you might want to record in your journal:

   a. Your thoughts
   b. Prayers
   c. Answers you have seen to prayers
   d. Things you have learned
   e. Progress (or lack thereof) you have made

6. Select an accountability partner.

"Two are better than one, because they have a good reward for their labor. For if they fall, one will lift up his companion. But

woe to him who is alone when he falls, for he has no one to help him up." (Ecclesiastes 4:9)

a. An accountability partner

1) Helps clarify goals. Sharing your goals with someone moves you towards achieving them.

2) Offers encouragement. A partner encourages you to keep moving towards your goals.

3) Challenges you. There may be times when you need a little "tough love". A partner reminds you of what you are working towards and how it will change your life.

b. What to look for when selecting an accountability partner.

1) Trust. Select someone that you trust. Otherwise, you will never get the full benefits of the relationship.

2) Honesty. Select someone who will be completely honest with you.

3) Confidentiality. Select someone who will keep all information discussed the two of you, without any exceptions.

4) Non-judgmental. Select someone who understands that their role is to listen, ask questions and offer feedback, but never to judge.

5) Common Core Beliefs. Select someone who shares your beliefs. For example, if you believe it is possible to control your feelings by controlling your thinking, your accountability partner should believe the same thing.

c. Get the maximum benefit from the partnership.

1) Be clear on your goal(s).

2) Meet with your partner (face-to-face or by telephone) once per week for three weeks.

3) Make notes in your journal on progress so you can follow-up at the next meeting.

4) Keep the commitment to meet on the agreed-upon date at the agreed-upon time.

7. Draw inspiration from a man who chose to rejoice despite a difficult boss.

Jerry had an awful boss (Carl) when he worked at a bank.

Carl was verbally abusive and condescending. Any time one of the employees made a suggestion, he immediately disregarded it without even considering it. Many employees quit or transferred to other departments. Those who remained talked about Carl behind his back and avoided him like the plague. Initially, Jerry followed the same approach.

Then, Jerry started having second thoughts. Since his dad had been a manager, he knew something about what managers go through. They face enormous pressure and sometimes they pass it on to employees. Jerry began to reflect on Scriptures he had learned, such as "Bear with one another, and forgive one another." (Colossians 3:13)

So, Jerry put his thoughts of transfer on hold and decided to use a Biblical approach:

a. He met with Carl. "If a brothers sins against you, go and tell him alone." (Matthew 18:15)

Jerry decided that rather than complaining to others, he would go to Carl and respectfully try and have a civil conversation. Jerry assured Carl that he was committed to helping him get what he needed. In order to do that he needed to clearly understand Carl's expectations. Surprisingly, Carl was open to this approach and he gave Jerry specifics on what he was looking for.

   b. He accommodated Carl's style. "To the weak I became as weak, that I might win the weak. I have become all things to all men, that I might by all means save some." (1 Corinthians 9:22)

For example, Jerry learned that Carl was a detail-oriented person. Even though Jerry was a big picture guy, he made sure that whenever he gave status reports to Carl, he gave him a lot more details than what he would normally have done. Jerry also asked Carl if there were any projects that he was doing personally that Jerry could take over. Carl gave Jerry two projects. One was representing him at a regularly scheduled meeting. Jerry made sure he gave Carl a detailed report, in writing, after each meeting. Carl told Jerry he really appreciated him doing this because it allowed him to devote more time to other issues that required his attention.

Jerry also adapted to Carl's method of communicating. Jerry preferred face to face communication. Carl preferred to communicate by email. So, Jerry communicated with Carl exclusively by email, unless he requested otherwise.

Jerry realized that Carl was an absolute stickler for meeting deadlines. So, Jerry made sure he met every deadline. If he found that he was going to need more time, he would let Carl know well in advance. Then, they would negotiate a new deadline, or Carl would give Jerry permission to re-prioritize his workload in order to meet the original deadline.

   c. Jerry sought to excel in everything he did. "Whatever you do, do it heartily, as to the Lord and not to men, knowing that from the Lord you will receive the reward of the inheritance; for you serve the Lord Christ." (Colossians 3:23-24)

Since Jerry knew that God was his ultimate boss, he made sure that all of his work was excellent. Having learned Carl's expectations, he endeavored to exceed all of them.

d. Jerry prayed for Carl regularly. "Love your enemies, bless those who curse you, do good to those who hate you, and pray for those who spitefully use you and persecute you." (Matthew 5:44-45)

Summary: By praying and following God's word, Jerry turned a very negative experience into a positive one. In fact, he says he learned an awful lot and grew in his faith and as an employee.

8. Draw inspiration from how God brought you through a previous problem.

"Remember how the LORD your God led you all the way in the wilderness these forty years, to humble and test you in order to know what was in your heart, whether or not you would keep his commands. He humbled you, causing you to hunger and then feeding you with manna, which neither you nor your ancestors had known, to teach you that man does not live on bread alone but on every word that comes from the mouth of the LORD. Your clothes did not wear out and your feet did not swell during these forty years." (Deuteronomy 8:2-4)

a. List a problem that you had in the past.

b. Describe how God brought you through it.

9. Guard against negative statements/questions.

"We demolish arguments and every pretension that sets itself up against the knowledge of God, and we take captive every thought to make it obedient to Christ." (2 Corinthians 10:5)

Since you have grown accustomed to making negative statements/questions to yourself about your difficult boss, you will be inclined to continue doing so. When you are tempted, ask yourself, "Is this statement/question aligned with what God says?" If not, immediately replace it with a verse from today's passage in Step 3.

Chapter Four

I Was Passed over for Promotion

SEEING COLLEAGUES PROMOTED while you are passed over can be unpleasant, particularly if you believe you are more qualified than the promoted colleagues. Yet, being passed over for promotion cannot steal your joy. What you choose to say to yourself about being passed over for promotion can. Why? What you choose to say to yourself determines how you feel. For example, if you tell yourself, "I will never get promoted" you will feel sad and disappointed. On the other hand, if you tell yourself, "I will be satisfied whether I get promoted or not" you will be able to rejoice.

You cannot control whether less qualified colleagues are promoted while you are passed over. You can control what you say to yourself. In order to rejoice, you must replace the negative statements/questions that you say to yourself. These nine steps will help you accomplish that:

1. **Examine typical negative statements/questions that people say to themselves:**

    "I am more qualified than the person they promoted."
    "I guess I don't measure up to the others who were promoted."
    "I was counting on the promotion to help meet my financial obligations."
    "I am done. I am going to look for another job."

2. List negative statements/questions that you say to yourself in the left column below:

Negative statements/ questions	Replace each with a verse from today's passage in Step 3

3. Meditate* on today's passage for 15 minutes per day for the next 21 days.

"Fix these words of mine in your hearts and minds; tie them as symbols on your hands and bind them on your foreheads. Teach them to your children, talking about them when you sit at home and when you walk along the road, when you lie down and when you get up." (Deuteronomy 11:18-19)

Day	Today's Passage
1	Psalm 75:6-7
2	Luke 19:17
3	Matthew 6:33
4	Hebrews 13:5
5	Jeremiah 29:11
6	2 Corinthians 5:20
7	Psalm 34:19
8	Psalm 139:14
9	Philippians 4:19
10	Matthew 6:31-33
11	Philippians 4:11
12	Colossians 3:23
13	Ecclesiastes 9:10
14	1 Thessalonians 5:17
15	Matthew 5:16
16	Matthew 5:12
17	1 Peter 4:13
18	Psalm 37:4
19	1 Thessalonians 5:18
20	James 1:2
21	Proverbs 17:22

*When I say "meditate" I do not mean incantations or lotus postures. Instead, I mean a time where you block out busy routines – prayer lists, study requirements, etc.

    a. Read the verse out loud two times.
    b. What does the verse mean to you now that you were passed over for promotion?
    c. Do I believe the verse with your mind and your heart?
    d. How will you think differently?
    e. How will you act differently?
    f. Memorize the verse.

Everyone wants to rejoice. But that can seem like mission impossible when you have been passed over for promotion. However, meditating on the verses in Step 3 for 15 minutes per day for 21 days will give you victory over your negative statements/questions. Then, you will be able to rejoice in the Lord.

4. Replace each negative statement/question you listed in Step 2 with a verse from today's passage in Step 3.

For example, replace: "I was counting on the promotion to help meet my financial obligations."

With: "My God shall supply all my need according to His riches in glory by Christ Jesus." (Philippians 4:19)

5. Keep a journal.

The Lord gave me this answer, "Write down clearly what I reveal to you." (Habakkuk 2:2)

Some things you might want to record in your journal:

a. Your thoughts
b. Prayers
c. Answers you have seen to prayers
d. Things you have learned
e. Progress (or lack thereof) you have made

6. Select an accountability partner.

"Two are better than one, because they have a good reward for their labor. For if they fall, one will lift up his companion. But woe to him who is alone when he falls, for he has no one to help him up." (Ecclesiastes 4:9)

a. An accountability partner

1) Help clarify goals. Sharing your goals with someone moves you towards achieving them.

2) Offers encouragement. A partner encourages you to keep moving towards your goals.

3) Challenges you. There may be times when you need a little "tough love". A partner reminds you of what you are working towards and how it will change your life.

b. What to look for when selecting an accountability partner.

1) Trust. Select someone that you trust. Otherwise, you will never get the full benefits of the relationship.

2) Honesty. Select someone who will be completely honest with you.

3) Confidentiality. Select someone who will keep all information discussed between the two of you, without any exceptions.

4) Non-judgmental. Select someone who understands that their role is to listen, ask questions and offer feedback, but never to judge.

5) Common Core Beliefs. Select someone who shares your beliefs. For example, if you believe it is possible to control your feelings by controlling your thinking, your accountability partner must believe the same thing.

c. Get the maximum benefit from the partnership.

1) Be clear on your goal(s).

2) Meet with your partner (face-to-face or by telephone) once per week for three weeks.

3) Make notes in your journal on progress so you can follow-up at the next meeting.

4) Keep the commitment to meet on the agreed-upon date at the agreed-upon time.

7. Draw inspiration from a woman who chose to rejoice despite being passed over for promotion.

Katrina was promised a promotion almost two years ago. Yet, it never happened. As a result, she became angry and frustrated. Her frustration and anger grew as she saw people who were not nearly as qualified getting promoted ahead of her.

She was about to confront her bosses when a friend from church told her that he had learned that when things like this had happened in his life, it meant that either God had some other plans for him, or that God knew he was ready to handle it. Katrina's friend went on to say that, as a result, he was learning to trust that God had a plan and that He knew what was best.

Although still feeling confrontational, Katrina turned to prayer and reading her Bible. Four truths stood out:

a. God is sovereign – He has complete control over everything.

"Remember the former things of old, for I am God, and there is no other; I am God, and there is none like me. Declaring the end from the beginning, and from ancient times things that are not yet done, saying, "My counsel shall stand, and I will do all my pleasure. Calling a bird of prey from the east, the man who executes my counsel, from a far country. Indeed, I have spoken it; I will also bring it to pass. I have purposed it; I will also do it." (Isaiah 46:9-11)

b. God even has control over who gets promoted.

"Promotion comes neither from the east nor the west nor from the south. But God is the judge; He puts down one and exalts another." (Psalm 75:6-7)

c. God has a plan for our life.

"For I know the plans I have for you," declares the Lord, "plans to prosper you and not to harm you, plans to give you hope and a future." (Jeremiah 29:11)

d. We are to trust God.

"Trust in the Lord with all year heart, and lean not on your own understanding; in all your ways acknowledge Him, and He shall direct your path." (Proverbs 3:5-6)

Although she still has not gotten promoted, Katrina's frustration and anger have given way to joy. She is content to do the very best job she can do and trust God for the promotion when and if He deems it appropriate.

Summary: By replacing her negative self-talk with God's word, Katrina went from being angry at her bosses and jealous of her colleagues to being content.

8. Draw inspiration from how God brought you through a previous problem.

"Remember how the LORD your God led you all the way in the wilderness these forty years, to humble and test you in order to know what was in your heart, whether or not you would keep his commands. He humbled you, causing you to hunger and then feeding you with manna, which neither you nor your ancestors had known, to teach you that man does not live on bread alone but on every word that comes from the mouth of the LORD. Your clothes did not wear out and your feet did not swell during these forty years." (Deuteronomy 8:2-4)

a. List a problem that you had in the past.

b. Describe how God brought you through it.

9. Guard against negative statements/questions.

"We demolish arguments and every pretension that sets itself up against the knowledge of God, and we take captive every thought to make it obedient to Christ." (2 Corinthians 10:5)

Since you have grown accustomed to making negative statements/questions to yourself about being passed over for promotion, you will be inclined to continue doing so. When you are tempted, ask yourself, "Is this statement/question aligned with what God says?" If not, immediately replace it with a verse from today's passage in Step 3.

Chapter Five

I Was Forced to Take a Pay Cut

ALTHOUGH TAKING A PAY CUT is common today, it cannot steal your joy. What you choose to say to yourself about taking a pay cut can. Why? What you choose to say to yourself determines how you feel. For example, if you tell yourself, "It is very unfair to have to take a pay cut" you will feel down. On the other hand, if tell yourself, "Despite the pay cut, I still have everything I need" you will be able to rejoice.

You cannot control whether you take a pay cut. You can control what you say to yourself. In order to rejoice, you must replace the negative statements/questions that you say to yourself. These nine steps will help you accomplish that:

1. **Examine typical negative statements/questions that people say to themselves:**

   "How am I going to meet my household expenses?"
   "I will quit and find another job."
   "The executives did not take a pay cut."
   "It is not fair."
   "I was expecting a pay raise, not a pay cut."

2. List negative statements/questions that you say to yourself the left column below:

Negative statements/ questions	Replace each with a verse from today's passage in Step 3

3. Meditate* on today's passage for 15 minutes per day for the next 21 days.

"Fix these words of mine in your hearts and minds; tie them as symbols on your hands and bind them on your foreheads. Teach them to your children, talking about them when you sit at home and when you walk along the road, when you lie down and when you get up." (Deuteronomy 11:18-19)

Day	Today's Passage
1	Philippians 4:19
2	Psalm 34:19
3	Romans 12:6
4	Proverbs 3:5-6
5	James 1:2
6	Psalm 37:4
7	Hebrews 13:5
8	Colossians 3:23
9	Ecclesiastes 9:10
10	John 6:27
11	Ephesians 6:5-8
12	1 Timothy 6:7-10
13	Jeremiah 29:11
14	Luke 3:14
15	Hebrews 13:5
16	2 Corinthians 5:20
17	Philippians 4:11
18	1 Peter 2:18
19	Matthew 6:24
20	Philippians 3:13
21	1 Thessalonians 5:17

*When I say "meditate" I do not mean incantations or lotus postures. Instead, I mean a time where you block out busy routines – prayer lists, study requirements, etc.

    a. Read the verse out loud two times.
    b. What does the verse mean to you now that you were forced to take a pay cut?
    c. Do you believe the verse with your mind and your heart?
    d. How will you think differently?
    e. How will you act differently?
    f. Memorize the verse.

Everyone wants to rejoice. But that can seem like mission impossible when you have been forced to take a pay cut. However, meditating on the verses in Step 3 for 15 minutes per day for 21 days will give you victory over your negative statements/questions. Then, you will be able to rejoice in the Lord.

4. Replace each negative statement/question you listed in Step 2 with a verse from today's passage in step 3.

For example, replace: "The executives did not take a pay cut."

With: "I have learned whatever state I am in, to be content." (Philippians 4:11)

5. Keep a journal.

The Lord gave me this answer, "Write down clearly what I reveal to you." (Habakkuk 2:2)

Some things you might want to record in your journal:

  a. Your thoughts
  b. Prayers
  c. Answers you have seen to prayers
  d. Things you have learned
  e. Progress (or lack thereof) you have made

6. Select an accountability partner.

"Two are better than one, because they have a good reward for their labor. For if they fall, one will lift up his companion. But woe to him who is alone when he falls, for he has no one to help him up." (Ecclesiastes 4:9)

a. An accountability partner

1) Helps clarify goals. Sharing your goals with someone moves you towards achieving them.

2) Offers encouragement. A partner encourages you to keep moving towards your goals.

3) Challenges you. There may be times when you need a little "tough love". A partner reminds you of what you are working towards and how it will change your life.

b. What to look for when selecting an accountability partner.

1) Trust. Select someone that you trust. Otherwise, you will never get the full benefits of the relationship.

2) Honesty. Select someone who will be completely honest with you.

3) Confidentiality. Select someone who will keep all information discussed between the two of you, without any exceptions.

4) Non-judgmental. Select someone who understands that their role is to listen, ask questions and offer feedback, but never to judge.

5) Common Core Beliefs. Select someone who shares your beliefs. For example, if you believe it is possible to control your feelings by controlling your thinking, your accountability partner must believe the same thing.

c. Get the maximum benefit from the partnership.

1) Be clear on your goal(s).

2) Meet with your partner (face-to-face or by telephone) once per week for three weeks.

3) Make notes in your journal on progress so you can follow-up at the next meeting.

4) Keep the commitment to meet on the agreed-upon date at the agreed-upon time.

7. Draw inspiration from a man who chose to rejoice despite being forced to take a pay cut.

Paul has been working for his employer for more than 10 years. Each year, he has gotten a pay increase. Last month his supervisor informed him that he not going to get a pay increase, and that he was going to have to take a five percent pay cut. His supervisor blames it on the economy.

Paul felt insulted. This was a horrible thing to have to swallow. He immediately thought about looking for another job. With his skills he was confident that he could find a better-paying job.

However, after talking with his wife, Paul calmed down a bit. He began having additional thoughts:

a. Unemployment was around 8 percent. So, finding a better opportunity may not be as easy as it has been in the past.

b. He liked the company for which he was working. His position matches the gifts God had given him.

c. He had built some deep relationships over the years and he had seen God working in the lives of his coworkers as a result of those relationships.

d. He was an ambassador for Christ. (2 Corinthians 5:20) Paul realized that his fellow employees were watching to see how he reacted to the pay cut.

e. He could free up extra cash by cutting some expenses.

f. God would meet his needs. "My God shall supply all your needs according to His riches in Christ Jesus." (Philippians 4:19)

Paul concluded that, even if it means no pay increase for this year and a temporary pay cut, this is where God wants him. He decided to not confront his bosses and to joyfully serve God where he is, rather than seek other opportunities.

Summary: Paul came to this conclusion because he listened to God's word instead of his own negative self-talk.

8. Draw inspiration from how God brought you through a previous problem.

"Remember how the LORD your God led you all the way in the wilderness these forty years, to humble and test you in order to know what was in your heart, whether or not you would keep his commands. He humbled you, causing you to hunger and then feeding you with manna, which neither you nor your ancestors had known, to teach you that man does not live on bread alone but on every word that comes from the mouth of the LORD. Your clothes did not wear out and your feet did not swell during these forty years." (Deuteronomy 8:2-4)

a. List a problem that you had in the past.

b. Describe how God brought you through it.

9. Guard against negative statements/questions.

"We demolish arguments and every pretension that sets itself up against the knowledge of God, and we take captive every thought to make it obedient to Christ." (2 Corinthians 10:5)

Since you have grown accustomed to making negative statements/questions to yourself about being forced to take a pay cut, you will be inclined to continue doing so. When you are tempted, ask yourself, "Is this statement/question aligned with what God says?" If not, immediately replace it with a verse from today's passage in Step 3.

Part Two

PHYSICAL HEALTH
PROBLEMS

Chapter Six

I Have Cancer

ACCORDING TO THE AMERICAN CANCER SOCIETY, approximately 12 million people are living with cancer in the U.S. Although living with cancer can be challenging, it cannot steal your joy. What you choose to say to yourself about living with cancer can. Why? What you say to yourself determines how you feel. For example, if you say to yourself, "Why did I have to get cancer?" you will feel down. On the other hand, if you say to yourself, "Cancer is not going to get me down" you will be able to rejoice.

You cannot control whether you get cancer. You can control what you say to yourself. In order to rejoice, you must replace the negative statements/questions that you say to yourself. These nine steps will help you accomplish that:

1. **Examine typical negative statements/questions that people say to themselves:**

   "I am worried."
   "I am discouraged."
   "I am afraid of how this is going to turn out."
   "Why me?"
   "The chemotherapy is difficult."

2. **List negative statements/questions that you say to yourself in the left column below:**

Negative statements/ questions	Replace each with a verse from today's passage in Step 3

3. Meditate* on today's passage for 15 minutes per day for the next 21 days.

"Fix these words of mine in your hearts and minds; tie them as symbols on your hands and bind them on your foreheads. Teach them to your children, talking about them when you sit at home and when you walk along the road, when you lie down and when you get up." (Deuteronomy 11:18-19)

Day	Today's Passage
1	Philippians 4:6
2	1 Peter 5:7
3	Isaiah 43:2
4	2 Corinthians 4:17-18
5	Matthew 17:20
6	Psalm 42:11
7	Psalm 118:24
8	Jeremiah 29:11
9	Job 2:10
10	Romans 8:38-39
11	Deuteronomy 31:8
12	Psalm 34:19
13	Psalm 37:4
14	Psalm 32:10
15	Psalm 50:15
16	Psalm 121:1-2
17	2 Corinthians 12:9
18	Joshua 1:5
19	Psalm 55:22
20	Romans 8:18
21	1 Thessalonians 5:17

*When I say "meditate" I do not mean incantations or lotus postures. Instead, I mean a time where you block out busy routines – prayer lists, study requirements, etc.

   a. Read the verse out loud two times.
   b. What does the verse mean to you now that you have cancer?
   c. Do you believe the verse with your mind and your heart?
   d. How will you think differently?
   e. How will you act differently?

    f. Memorize the verse.

Everyone wants to rejoice. But that can seem like mission impossible when you have cancer. However, meditating on the verses in Step 3 for 15 minutes per day for 21 days will give you victory over your negative statements/questions. Then, you will be able to rejoice in the Lord.

4. Replace each negative statement/question you listed in Step 2 with a verse from today's passage in Step 3.

For example, replace: "Why me?"

With: "Shall we accept good from God, and not trouble?" (Job 2:10)

5. Keep a journal.

The Lord gave me this answer, "Write down clearly what I reveal to you." (Habakkuk 2:2)

Some things you might want to record in your journal:

    a. Your thoughts
    b. Prayers
    c. Answers you have seen to prayers
    d. Things you have learned
    e. Progress (or lack thereof) you have made

6. Select an accountability partner.

"Two are better than one, because they have a good reward for their labor. For if they fall, one will lift up his companion. But woe to him who is alone when he falls, for he has no one to help him up." (Ecclesiastes 4:9)

a. An accountability partner

1) Helps clarify goals. Sharing your goals with someone moves you towards achieving them.

2) Offers encouragement. A partner encourages you to keep moving towards your goals.

3) Challenges you. There may be times when you need a little "tough love". A partner reminds you of what you are working towards and how it will change your life.

b. What to look for when selecting an accountability partner.

1) Trust. Select someone that you trust. Otherwise, you will never get the full benefits of the relationship.

2) Honesty. Select someone who will be completely honest with you.

3) Confidentiality. Select someone who will keep all information discussed between the two of you, without any exceptions.

4) Non-judgmental. Select someone who understands that their role is to listen, ask questions and offer feedback, but never to judge.

5) Common Core Beliefs. Select someone who shares your beliefs. For example, if you believe it is possible to control your feelings by controlling your thinking, your accountability partner must believe the same thing.

c. Get the maximum benefit from the partnership.

1) Be clear on your goal(s).

2) Meet with your partner (face-to-face or by telephone) once per week for three weeks.

3) Make notes in your journal on progress so you can follow-up at the next meeting.

4) Keep the commitment to meet on the agreed-upon date at the agreed-upon time.

7. Draw inspiration from someone who chose to rejoice despite having cancer.

After undergoing some tests, Marilyn received the dreaded news – she had cancer.

At first, she was in disbelief. This was followed by many questions ... "How did I get cancer?" I never smoked." "I'm only 31 years old." "Why was I just promoted to an account executive position if I was going to get cancer?" "Am I going to die?" "Will I not be able to get married and have lots of babies?" "Where is God?"

Since the tumor was so advanced, the surgeon said they needed to remove as much of it as was visible. After surgery, Marilyn would need to undergo aggressive chemotherapy.

She asked members of her church and her family to pray for her and the surgical team.

The doctors were pleased with the surgical results and Marilyn began chemotherapy. After the first few treatments, she was feeling the effects of the chemotherapy. However, the tumor had not shrunk. She cried out to God "How much more can I take?" She prayed and meditated on several verses:

a. "We must through many tribulations enter the kingdom of God." (Acts 14:22)

b. "Be anxious for nothing, but in everything by prayer and supplication, with thanksgiving, let your requests be made known to God; and the peace of God, which surpasses all understanding, will guard your hearts and minds through Christ Jesus." (Philippians 4:6)

c. "Humble yourselves under the mighty hand of God, that He may exalt you in due time, casting all your care upon Him, for He cares for you." (1 Peter 5:6-7)

d. "Many are the afflictions of the righteous, but the Lord delivers him out of them all." (Psalm 34:1)

e. "For our light affliction, which is but for a moment, is working for us a far more exceeding and eternal weight in glory, while we do not look at the things which are seen, but at the things which are not seen. For the things which are seen are temporary, but the things which are not seen are eternal." (2 Corinthians 4:17-18)

f. "For I know the plans I have for you, declares the Lord, plans for welfare and not for evil, to give you a future and a hope." (Jeremiah 29:11)

g. "For I am persuaded that neither death nor life, nor angels nor principalities nor powers, nor things present nor things to come, nor height nor depth, nor any other created thing, shall be able to separate us from the love of God which is in Christ Jesus our Lord." (Romans 8:38-39)

h. "And the Lord, He is the One who goes before you. He will be with you, He will not leave you nor forsake you; do not fear or be afraid." (Deuteronomy 31:8)

i. "The righteous cry out, and the Lord hears and delivers them out of all their troubles." (Psalm 34:17)

These verses, along with prayers, helped Marilyn go from sadness to joy. Despite still experiencing the effects of the treatments, she began offering encouragement to others who were receiving chemotherapy. This not only helped them, but helped her, as well.

After five months of grueling chemotherapy, three blood transfusions, losing 45 pounds, achy joints, hair loss, mouth sores, and numbness in her fingers and toes, Marilyn's latest computed tomography (CT) scan showed no signs of cancer.

Summary: Relying on God's word allowed Marilyn to change her self-talk. As a result she went from being afraid of dying and feeling sorry for herself to rejoicing and encouraging others who were living with cancer.

8. Draw inspiration from how God brought you through a previous problem.

"Remember how the Lord your God led you all the way in the wilderness these forty years, to humble and test you in order to know what was in your heart, whether or not you would keep his commands. He humbled you, causing you to hunger and then feeding you with manna, which neither you nor your ancestors had known, to teach you that man does not live on bread alone but on every word that comes from the mouth of the Lord. Your clothes did not wear out and your feet did not swell during these forty years." (Deuteronomy 8:2-4)

a. List a problem that you had in the past.

b. Describe how God brought you through it.

9. Guard against negative statements/questions.

"We demolish arguments and every pretension that sets itself up against the knowledge of God, and we take captive every thought to make it obedient to Christ." (2 Corinthians 10:5)

Since you have grown accustomed to making negative statements/questions to yourself about having cancer, you will be inclined to continue doing so. When you are tempted, ask yourself, "Is this statement/question aligned with what God says?" If not, immediately replace it with a verse from today's passage in Step 3.

Chapter Seven

I Have a Terminal Illness

HAVING A TERMINAL ILLNESS cannot steal your joy. What you choose to say to yourself about having a terminal illness can. Why? What you choose to say to yourself determines how you feel. For example, if you tell yourself, "It is hopeless" you will feel down. On the other hand, if you tell yourself "I am going to spend an eternity with Jesus" you will be able to rejoice.

You cannot control whether you get a terminal illness. You can control what you say to yourself. In order to rejoice, you must replace the negative statements/questions that you say to yourself. These nine steps will help you accomplish that:

1. **Examine typical negative statements/questions that people say to themselves:**

   "The doctor said I have six months to live."
   "I worry about how my family will make it if I die."
   "I am scared."
   "I wonder what lies beyond this life."
   "Why me?

2. **List negative statements/questions that you say to yourself in the left column below:**

Negative statements/ questions	Replace each with a verse from today's passage in Step 3

3. **Meditate* on today's passage for 15 minutes per day for the next 21 days.**

"Fix these words of mine in your hearts and minds; tie them as symbols on your hands and bind them on your foreheads. Teach them to your children, talking about them when you sit at home and when you walk along the road, when you lie down and when you get up." (Deuteronomy 11:18-19)

Day	Today's Passage
1	Psalm 73:26
2	Romans 3:23
3	Romans 6:23
4	Ephesians 2:8-9
5	John 3:16
6	Romans 10:9
7	Philippians 1:21
8	1 Corinthians 3:21-23
9	Luke 1:37
10	Romans 8:28
11	2 Corinthians 4:16
12	Luke 23:43
13	2 Timothy 4:6-8
14	Luke 12:8
15	John 11:25
16	John 14:1-3
17	Revelation 21:4
18	Psalm 16:11
19	Isaiah 49:14-16
20	John 12:26
21	1 Thessalonians 5:17

*When I say "meditate" I do not mean incantations or lotus postures. Instead, I mean a time where you block out busy routines – prayer lists, study requirements, etc.

    a. Read the verse out loud two times.
    b. What does the verse mean to you now that you have a terminal illness?
    c. Do you believe the verse with your mind and your heart?
    d. How will you think differently?
    e. How will you act differently?
    f. Memorize the verse.

Everyone wants to rejoice. But that can seem like mission impossible when you have a terminal illness. However, meditating on the verses in Step 3 for 15 minutes per day for 21 days will give you victory over your negative statements/ questions. Then, you will be able to rejoice in the Lord.

4. Replace each negative statement/question you listed in Step 2 with a verse from today's passage in Step 3.

For example, replace: "The doctor said I have six months to live."

With: "My flesh and my heart fail; but God is the strength of my heart and my portion forever." (Psalm 73:26)

5. Keep a journal.

The Lord gave me this answer, "Write down clearly what I reveal to you." (Habakkuk 2:2)

Some things you might want to record in your journal:

a. Your thoughts
b. Prayers
c. Answers you have seen to prayers
d. Things you have learned
e. Progress (or lack thereof) you have made

6. Select an accountability partner.

"Two are better than one, because they have a good reward for their labor. For if they fall, one will lift up his companion. But woe to him who is alone when he falls, for he has no one to help him up." (Ecclesiastes 4:9)

a. An accountability partner

1) Helps clarify goals. Sharing your goals with someone moves you towards achieving them.

2) Offers encouragement. A partner encourages you to keep moving towards your goals.

3) Challenges you. There may be times when you need a little "tough love". A partner reminds you of what you are working towards and how it will change your life.

b. What to look for when selecting an accountability partner.

1) Trust. Select someone that you trust. Otherwise, you will never get the full benefits of the relationship.

2) Honesty. Select someone who will be completely honest with you.

3) Confidentiality. Select someone who will keep all information discussed between the two of you, without any exceptions.

4) Non-judgmental. Select someone who understands that their role is to listen, ask questions and offer feedback, but never to judge.

5) Common Core Beliefs. Select someone who shares your beliefs. For example, if you believe it is possible to control your feelings by controlling your thinking, your accountability partner must believe the same thing.

c. Get the maximum benefit from the partnership.

1) Be clear on your goal(s).

2) Meet with your partner (face-to-face or by telephone) once per week for three weeks.

3) Make notes in your journal on progress so you can follow-up at the next meeting.

4) Keep the commitment to meet on the agreed-upon date at the agreed-upon time.

7. Draw inspiration from someone who chose to rejoice despite having a terminal illness.

When Michael Budd landed in the hospital in August 1991, he said he had pneumonia. A few days later his family learned that he had AIDS. At one point, Michael was extremely angry. However, that only lasted a short time, and he apologized for his outbursts. Then he accepted the fact that he had AIDS and, reluctantly and fearfully, that he was going to die.

Michael thought that he could somehow do enough good that God would be willing to accept him into heaven.

A family member explained to him that the only way to heaven was to:

- "Admit that you are a sinner." - Romans 3:23
- "Realize that the penalty of sin is eternal death." - Romans 6:23a
- "Acknowledge that there is nothing you can do to save yourself." - Romans 3:20
- "Realize that Christ has paid the penalty for sin." - Romans 5:8-9
- "Believe in Jesus Christ alone for salvation." - Romans 10:9

Within a week, Michael accepted Christ as his savior. Instead of thinking he had to earn his way to heaven, he had accepted the free gift that God offers to everyone who believes in Him.

Instead of dreading dying, Michael began looking forward to being with Jesus, his father and his beloved grandmother. He recognized, as Philippians 1:21 says: "For to me, to live is Christ, and to die is gain."

Michael enjoyed having family members read the Bible to him. Some of his favorite verses were:

a. "In your presence is fullness of joy. At your right hand are pleasures forevermore. (Psalm 16:11)

b. "We do not lose heart. Even though our outward man is perishing, yet the inward man is being renewed day by day." (2 Corinthians 4:16)

c. "Our light affliction, which is but for a moment, is working for us a far more exceeding and eternal weight of glory, while we do not look at the things which are seen, but at the things which are not seen. For the things which are seen are temporary, but the things which are not seen are eternal." (2 Corinthians 4:17-18)

d. "I consider that the sufferings of this present time are not worthy to be compared with the glory which shall be revealed in us." (Romans 8:18)

e. "Confess your trespasses to one another." (James 5:16)

Michael called and apologized to each person against whom he felt he had committed an injustice. "Therefore confess your sins to each other and pray for each other so that you may be healed." (James 5:16)

Michael forgave anyone who had done an injustice to him, even though they did not ask. "Forgive one another, just as God in Christ also forgave you." (Ephesians 4:32)

During various times when he was in the hospital, Michael prayed with and for other patients. He also asked family members to go to other patients rooms and pray with them. "Serve one another in love." (Galatians 5:13)

In addition, he told his family of other people he knew who had AIDS. His family would later minister to these folks and their families through The Michael Budd Foundation for AIDS Support.

Towards the end of his time on earth, Michael planned his funeral.

He selected the clothes in which he wanted to be buried and the songs he wanted sung. He met with his pastor to get approval to have the service at a larger, one-story church in order to make it easier for older members to attend. He requested that his body be placed in the church early so people who were not able to attend the service could view it. Finally, he requested that the pastor share the gospel message and invite people in attendance to receive Jesus Christ as their Lord and Savior.

Summary: Michael changed his self-talk. As a result he went from being afraid of dying and feeling like he had to earn his salvation, to accepting the free gift of being saved through Jesus' death and resurrection. Having done that, he became a missionary crusading to bring others into a relationship with Christ.

8. Draw inspiration from how God brought you through a previous problem.

"Remember how the LORD your God led you all the way in the wilderness these forty years, to humble and test you in order to know what was in your heart, whether or not you would keep his commands. He humbled you, causing you to hunger and then feeding you with manna, which neither you nor your ancestors had known, to teach you that man does not live on bread alone but on every word that comes from the mouth of the LORD. Your clothes did not wear out and your feet did not swell during these forty years." (Deuteronomy 8:2-4)

a. List a problem that you had in the past.

b. Describe how God brought you through it.

9. Guard against negative statements/questions.

"We demolish arguments and every pretension that sets itself up against the knowledge of God, and we take captive every thought to make it obedient to Christ." (2 Corinthians 10:5)

Since you have grown accustomed to making negative statements/questions to yourself about having a terminal illness, you will be inclined to continue doing so. When you are tempted, ask yourself, "Is this statement/question aligned with what God says?" If not, immediately replace it with a verse from today's passage in Step 3.

Chapter Eight

I Have a Chronic Illness

ACCORDING TO THE CENTER for Disease Control and Prevention, about 133 million Americans—nearly 1 in 2 adults—live with at least one chronic illness. Although living with a chronic illness presents challenges, it cannot steal your joy. What you choose to say to yourself about living with a chronic illness can. Why? What you say to yourself determines how you feel. For example, if you tell yourself, "Why me?" you will feel down. On the other hand, if you tell yourself "Lots of people are living productive lives with the same illness", you will be able to rejoice.

You cannot control whether you have a chronic illness. You can control what you say to yourself. In order to rejoice, you must replace the negative statements/questions that you say to yourself. These nine steps will help you accomplish that:

1. **Examine typical negative statements/questions that people say to themselves:**

   "Why me?"
   "God has forsaken me."
   "I am so tired of this."
   "I am so afraid of the progression of my illness."
   "I may not have everything I need."

2. List negative statements/questions that you say to yourself in the left column below:

Negative statements/ questions	Replace each with a verse from today's passage in Step 3

3. Meditate* on today's passage for 15 minutes per day for the next 21 days.

"Fix these words of mine in your hearts and minds; tie them as symbols on your hands and bind them on your foreheads. Teach them to your children, talking about them when you sit at home and when you walk along the road, when you lie down and when you get up." (Deuteronomy 11:18-19)

Day	Today's Passage
1	Acts 14:22
2	2 Corinthians 12:9
3	Romans 8:28
4	Ecclesiastes 7:14
5	2 Corinthians 4:17-18
6	1 Peter 4:10
7	Psalm 145:18-19
8	Isaiah 43:2
9	Exodus 33:14
10	Matthew 11:28
11	Romans 8:18
12	Psalm 9:9-10
13	Psalm 16:8
14	Psalm 34:4
15	Isaiah 41:10
16	Proverbs 18:10
17	Psalm 34:10
18	Matthew 6:31-33
19	Philippians 4:19
20	Psalm 42:5
21	1 Thessalonians 5:17

*When I say "meditate" I do not mean incantations or lotus postures. Instead, I mean a time where you block out busy routines – prayer lists, study requirements, etc.

   a. Read the verse out loud two times.
   b. What does the verse mean to you now that you have a chronic illness?
   c. Do you believe the verse with your mind and your heart?
   d. How will you think differently?
   e. How will you act differently?

f. Memorize the verse.

Everyone wants to rejoice. But that can seem like mission impossible when you have a chronic illness. However, meditating on the verses in Step 3 for 15 minutes per day for 21 days will give you victory over your negative statements/ questions. Then, you will be able to rejoice in the Lord.

4. Replace each negative statement/question you listed in Step 2 with a verse from today's passage in Step 3.

For example, replace: "I am so tired of this."

With: "Come to me, all you who labor and are heavy laden, I will give you rest." (Matthew 11:28)

5. Keep a journal.

The Lord gave me this answer, "Write down clearly what I reveal to you." (Habakkuk 2:2)

Some things you might want to record in your journal:

a. Your thoughts
b. Prayers
c. Answers you have seen to prayers
d. Things you have learned
e. Progress (or lack thereof) you have made

6. Select an accountability partner.

"Two are better than one, because they have a good reward for their labor. For if they fall, one will lift up his companion. But woe to him who is alone when he falls, for he has no one to help him up." (Ecclesiastes 4:9)

a. An accountability partner

1) Helps clarify goals. Sharing your goals with someone moves you towards achieving them.

2) Offers encouragement. A partner encourages you to keep moving towards your goals.

3) Challenges you. There may be times when you need a little "tough love". A partner reminds you of what you are working towards and how it will change your life.

b. What to look for when selecting an accountability partner.

1) Trust. Select someone that you trust. Otherwise, you will never get the full benefits of the relationship.

2) Honesty. Select someone who will be completely honest with you.

3) Confidentiality. Select someone who will keep all information discussed between the two of you, without any exceptions.

4) Non-judgmental. Select someone who understands that their role is to listen, ask questions and offer feedback, but never to judge.

5) Common Core Beliefs. Select someone who shares your beliefs. For example, if you believe it is possible to control your feelings by controlling your thinking, your accountability partner must believe the same thing.

c. Get the maximum benefit from the partnership.

1) Be clear on your goal(s).

2) Meet with your partner (face-to-face or by telephone) once per week for three weeks.

3) Make notes in your journal on progress so you can follow-up at the next meeting.

4) Keep the commitment to meet on the agreed-upon date at the agreed-upon time.

7. Draw inspiration from someone who chose to rejoice despite having a chronic illness.

My late wife, Gayle, was diagnosed with crohn's disease at the age of 27. She went to be with the Lord at the age of 57.

At the time of her diagnosis, her doctor indicated that he preferred to avoid treating the disease with prednisone because of the severe long term side effects. Although he tried several medications to control the disease, the only effective one was prednisone.

It was not long before Gayle began experiencing the first side effects – her immune system was suppressed. This resulted in her continually getting infections. These infections would land her in the hospital multiple times of the next 30 years.

Instead of being discouraged, she reflected on Jeremiah 29:11 "For I know the plans I have for you," declares the Lord, "plans to prosper you and not to harm you, plans to give you hope and a future."

Acting on 1 Peter 4:10: "Each one has received a gift, minister it to one another, as good stewards of the manifold grace of God," she used her gift of teaching to teach middle school Science for sixteen years. She was very dedicated to her students and was named outstanding teacher 2 years in a row.

Using her detail-oriented gifts, Gayle always sent birthday, get well and anniversary cards to friends and family. She also organized all family get-togethers and she helped senior citizens work through their medical bills. This gave them peace of mind and prevented them from paying bills that they did not need to pay.

In 1993 she was diagnosed with diabetes. She threw herself into learning as much as she could about the disease. Her knowledge enabled her to control her glucose level without insulin. She served others by writing an instructional package to help them manage their glucose level without taking insulin.

At her doctor's recommendation, she resigned from her teaching job in June 1987. However, she continued to teach in the church learning center and she co-led a Bible study for college kids. She also did bookkeeping and accounting for the family's home based business.

As time went on, Gayle developed additional side effects from the prednisone. These included rheumatoid arthritis, asthmatic bronchitis, cataracts, glaucoma, hypertension and finally, peripheral artery disease (PAD).

With so many hospital stays (once for 48 days), Gayle became well-known among the nurses. They sought her counsel on everything from recipes to relationships.

Since she had multiple chronic illnesses, she had instant credibility with others who had the same illnesses. She counseled several people on how to manage their illness and deal with health care providers. She also encouraged them to seek the Lord and His strength. "Blessed be the God and Father of our Lord Jesus Christ, the father of mercies and God of all comfort, who comforts us in all our tribulation, that we may be able to comfort those who are in tribulation, with the comfort with which we ourselves are comforted by God." (2 Corinthians 1:3-5)

Despite having three surgeries during 1991, Gayle helped take care of her brother, Michael Budd. (See Chapter 7 – I Have

Terminal Illness). She was instrumental in leading Michael into a relationship with Jesus Christ.

After Michael went to be with Jesus in September 1992, Gayle co- founded The Michael Budd Foundation for Aids Support. As treasurer, she helped raise funds to meet the financial needs of other persons living with AIDS. She also helped lead several young men to accept Jesus Christ as their Savior.

Through all of her illnesses, Gayle kept her joy. She laughed often about wanting to be an organ donor, but she was sure nobody would accept her organs. She joyfully looked forward to being in heaven where she would not need walkers, canes, wheelchairs, stair lifts and she would not have to take 45 pills each day or receive intravenous antibiotics. She also looked forward to being face to face with God and being reunited with her beloved grandmother, father and brother.

She found several verses to be particularly comforting:

a. "I have heard of you by the hearing of the ear, but now my eyes see you." (Job 42:5)

b. "Those who wait on the Lord shall renew their strength; they shall mount up with wings like eagles, they will run and not be weary, they shall walk and not faint." (Isaiah 40:31)

c. "For I am persuaded that neither death nor life, neither angels nor principalities nor powers, nor things present nor things to come, nor height nor depth, nor any other created thing, shall be able to separate us from the love of God which is in Christ Jesus our Lord." (Romans 8:38-39)

d. "I sought the Lord, and He heard me, and delivered me from all my fears." (Psalm 34:4)

Summary: Gayle put on the whole armor of God. As a result, she rejoiced as she focused on how she could use the knowledge she had gained through her health issues to serve others.

8. Draw inspiration from how God brought you through a previous problem.

"Remember how the LORD your God led you all the way in the wilderness these forty years, to humble and test you in order to know what was in your heart, whether or not you would keep his commands. He humbled you, causing you to hunger and then feeding you with manna, which neither you nor your ancestors had known, to teach you that man does not live on bread alone but on every word that comes from the mouth of the LORD. Your clothes did not wear out and your feet did not swell during these forty years." (Deuteronomy 8:2-4)

   a. List a problem that you had in the past.

   b. Describe how God brought you through it.

9. Guard against negative statements/questions.

"We demolish arguments and every pretension that sets itself up against the knowledge of God, and we take captive every thought to make it obedient to Christ." (2 Corinthians 10:5)

Since you have grown accustomed to making negative statements/questions to yourself about having a chronic illness, you will be inclined to continue doing so. When you are tempted, ask yourself, "Is this statement/question aligned with what God says?" If not, immediately replace it with a verse from today's passage in Step 3.

Chapter Nine

I Am Disabled

ACCORDING TO THE U.S Census Bureau, about one in five U.S. residents - 19 percent - reported some level of disability in 2005. Although being disabled can affect your life, it cannot steal your joy. What you choose to say to yourself about being disabled can. Why? What you choose to say to yourself determines how you feel. For example, if you tell yourself, "This is horrible what has happened to me" you will feel down. On the other hand, if you tell yourself, "Despite my disability, there are many things I can do well" you will be able to rejoice.

You cannot control whether you are disabled. You can control what you say to yourself. In order to rejoice, you must replace the negative statements/questions that you say to yourself. These nine steps will help you accomplish that:

1. Examine typical negative statements/questions that disabled people say to themselves:

"Why has God allowed this to happen to me?"
"I am so tired of being limited in what I can do."
"I am frustrated since I cannot do the things I used to do."
"I am afraid of what lies ahead."
"I am losing my faith."

2. **List negative statements/questions that you say to yourself in the left column below:**

Negative statements/ questions	Replace each with a verse from today's passage in Step 3

3. **Meditate* on today's passage for 15 minutes per day for the next 21 days.**

"Fix these words of mine in your hearts and minds; tie them as symbols on your hands and bind them on your foreheads. Teach them to your children, talking about them when you sit at home and when you walk along the road, when you lie down and when you get up." (Deuteronomy 11:18-19)

Day	Today's Passage
1	Psalm 22:24
2	Romans 8:28
3	Nehemiah 8:10
4	Psalm 34:19
5	2 Corinthians 4:17-18
6	1 Peter 4:10
7	2 Corinthians 12:9
8	1 Peter 5:7
9	Romans 8:18
10	James 1:5
11	2 Timothy 1:7
12	Isaiah 43:2
13	Philippians 4:19
14	Psalm 37:8
15	Hebrews 10:23
16	Romans 5:3-5
17	Isaiah 40:31
18	Psalm 55:22
19	Jeremiah 29:11
20	Psalm 121:1-2
21	1 Thessalonians 5:17

*When I say "meditate" I do not mean incantations or lotus postures. Instead, I mean a time where you block out busy routines – prayer lists, study requirements, etc.

a. Read the verse out loud two times.
b. What does the verse mean to you now that you are disabled?
c. Do you believe the verse with your mind and your heart?
d. How will you think differently?
e. How will you act differently?
f. Memorize the verse.

Everyone wants to rejoice. But that can seem like mission impossible when you are disabled. However, meditating on the verses in Step 3 for 15 minutes per day for 21 days will give you victory over your negative statements/questions. Then, you will be able to rejoice in the Lord.

4. Replace each negative statement/question you listed in Step 2 with a verse from today's passage in Step 3.

For example, replace: "Why has God allowed this to happen to me?"

With: "He has not despised nor abhorred the affliction of the afflicted; nor has He hidden His face from Him, but when He cried to Him, He heard." (Psalm 22:24)

5. Keep a journal.

The Lord gave me this answer, "Write down clearly what I reveal to you. (Habakkuk 2:2)

Some things you might want to record in your journal:

   a. Your thoughts
   b. Prayers
   c. Answers you have seen to prayers
   d. Things you have learned
   e. Progress (or lack thereof) you have made

6. Select an accountability partner.

"Two are better than one, because they have a good reward for their labor. For if they fall, one will lift up his companion. But woe to him who is alone when he falls, for he has no one to help him up." (Ecclesiastes 4:9)

a. An accountability partner

1) Helps clarify goals. Sharing your goals with someone moves you towards achieving them.

2) Offers encouragement. A partner encourages you to keep moving towards your goals.

3) Challenges you. There may be times when you need a little "tough love". A partner reminds you of what you are working towards and how it will change your life.

b. What to look for when selecting an accountability partner.

1) Trust. Select someone that you trust. Otherwise, you will never get the full benefits of the relationship.

2) Honesty. Select someone who will be completely honest with you.

3) Confidentiality. Select someone who will keep all information discussed between the two of you, without any exceptions.

4) Non-judgmental. Select someone who understands that their role is to listen, ask questions and offer feedback, but never to judge.

5) Common Core Beliefs. Select someone who shares your beliefs. For example, if you believe it is possible to control your feelings by controlling your thinking, your accountability partner must believe the same thing.

c. Get the maximum benefit from the partnership.

1) Be clear on your goal(s).

2) Meet with your partner (face-to-face or by telephone) once per week for three weeks.

3) Make notes in your journal on progress so you can follow-up at the next meeting.

4) Keep the commitment to meet on the agreed-upon date at the agreed-upon time.

7. Draw inspiration from two men who chose to rejoice despite being disabled.

Dave Dravecky was always an outstanding pitcher, even tossing a no-hitter for his high school team.

He continued his career at Youngstown State University. Upon graduation, the Pittsburg Pirates drafted him. Later, they traded him to the San Diego Padres. He made his major league debut in 1982.

Dravecky won 14 games in 1983 and represented the Padres at the All-Star game. Equally proficient as a starter or relief pitcher, Dravecky helped the Padres achieve their first pennant in 1984.

On July 4, 1987, the Padres traded Dravecky to the San Francisco Giants. He won 7 games and helped the Giants reach the playoffs. He was on top of the world. He had a terrific family and was enjoying incredible success living his childhood dream of being a major league pitcher. Dave says that, although he did not realize it at the time, baseball was simply a platform for his real purpose – sharing hope with those suffering around the world.

In 1988 doctors discovered a cancerous growth in Dravecky's pitching arm. He underwent surgery on October 7, 1988 to try to eliminate all of the cancerous cells. Doctors told Dave that, barring a miracle, he would never pitch again.

However, following months of rehabilitation, he was pitching in the minor leagues by July 1989. He returned to the major leagues on August 10, 1989. He pitched eight innings and defeated Cincinnati 4–3.

Five days later, Dravecky pitched three innings. Then, he felt a tingling sensation in his arm. In the sixth inning, on his first pitch, Dave's left arm snapped with a deafening crack that could be heard in the stands. His arm was broken.

The Giants went on to win the National League pennant in 1989. During the post-game celebration, Dravecky broke his arm a second time when he ran out to the mound to celebrate. While examining Dave's x-rays, doctors noticed a mass in his arm. The cancer had returned. Dave retired from baseball in November, 1989, at the age of 33, and in the prime of his career.

He underwent further surgery and radiation in 1990. During 1991, he was bedridden and experienced incessant pain caused by a severe staph infection. Finally, on June 18, 1991, surgeons amputated Dave's left arm, shoulder blade and left side of his collarbone for fear that the cancer would spread and take his life.

During an interview with USA today, Dravecky admitted to the mental challenges, depression and family strain that resulted from his amputation. He went on to say, however, that because of his faith in God "I've come to understand that God is really shaping and molding my character. I've come to understand that real growth of character takes place in the valleys of life."

Dave and Jan were encouraged by all the cards, letters they received during the time they were suffering.

Acting on 1 Corinthians 1:4," Comfort those who are going through any tribulation with the comfort with which we are comforted by God", Dave and Jan founded Endurance, a ministry to come along side those who are suffering, to offer encouragement and to let people know that God is with them in their suffering.

Dave is the author of *Comeback, Worth of a Man, Do not Lose heart, Called Up and When You Can't Come Back*

In addition to his books, Dave speaks to audiences around the country about his experiences. His goals are to demonstrate how God brought him through the tribulations and to offer hope and encouragement to suffering people.

Summary: Dave Dravecky changed his thinking and went from self-pity about his career being over at age 33, to thanking God for using baseball to give him a platform for sharing hope with those suffering around the world.

Dr. Henry Viscardi, Jr. was born in 1912 with stumps instead of legs. Overcoming tremendous odds, Viscardi graduated from high school and went to college. At the age of twenty-seven, Henry was able to utilize artificial limbs for the first time.

He became a pioneer of the disabled movement that revolutionized education, rehabilitation, and employment of the disabled. During World War II, he helped armless and legless veterans at Walter Reed Hospital adjust to their new challenges. He founded the National Center for Disability Services and the Henry Viscardi School for the Disabled. He traveled the world promoting his message: face the world boldly and always have hope.

8. Draw inspiration from how God brought you through a previous problem.

"Remember how the LORD your God led you all the way in the wilderness these forty years, to humble and test you in order to know what was in your heart, whether or not you would keep his commands. He humbled you, causing you to hunger and then feeding you with manna, which neither you nor your ancestors had known, to teach you that man does not live on bread alone but on every word that comes from the mouth of the LORD. Your clothes did not wear out and your feet did not swell during these forty years." (Deuteronomy 8:2-4)

a. List a problem that you had in the past.

b. Describe how God brought you through it.

9. Guard against negative statements/questions.

"We demolish arguments and every pretension that sets itself up against the knowledge of God, and we take captive every thought to make it obedient to Christ." (2 Corinthians 10:5)

Since you have grown accustomed to making negative statements/questions to yourself about being disabled, you will be inclined to continue doing so. When you are tempted, ask yourself, "Is this statement/question aligned with what God says?" If not, immediately replace it with a verse from today's passage in Step 3.

Part Three

EMOTIONAL HEALTH
PROBLEMS

Chapter Ten
I Worry Constantly

WORRYING IS a preoccupation with negative thoughts about past or future negative events. These thoughts are often characterized by the phrases "If only..." and "What if..." For example, "If only I hadn't smoked all those years" or "What if I run out of money and can't pay my bills." Past or future events cannot steal your joy. What you tell yourself about past or future events can. Why? What you say to yourself determines how you feel. If you tell yourself statements/questions like those above, you will feel down. On the other hand, if you tell yourself, "I am not going to worry about the past or the future" you will be able to rejoice.

You cannot control past or future events. You can control what you say to yourself. In order to rejoice, you must replace the negative statements/questions that you say to yourself. These nine steps will help you accomplish that:

1. **Examine typical negative statements/questions that people who worry say to themselves:**

   "The churning inside me never stops." (Job 30:27)
   "I do not have a husband to take care of me and I am afraid that I may not have enough income."
   "I don't think God can help me."
   "What if my unemployment benefits run out before I find another job?"
   "If only I had not resigned."

2. **List negative statements/questions that you say to yourself in the left column below:**

Negative statements/ questions	Replace each with a verse from today's passage in Step 3

3. **Meditate* on today's passage for 15 minutes per day for the next 21 days.**

"Fix these words of mine in your hearts and minds; tie them as symbols on your hands and bind them on your foreheads. Teach them to your children, talking about them when you sit at home and when you walk along the road, when you lie down and when you get up." (Deuteronomy 11:18-19)

Day	Today's Passage
1	Matthew 11:28
2	Philippians 4:6
3	1 Peter 5:7
4	Philippians 4:19
5	Isaiah 26:3
6	Matthew 6:31-34
7	Proverbs 3:5-6
8	Psalm 118:24
9	Ephesians 6:17
10	Mark 4:39
11	Psalm 23:1
12	2 Timothy 1:7
13	Psalm 34:19
14	1 Peter 5:8
15	James 4:7
16	Psalm 4:8
17	James 1:2
18	Psalm 55:22
19	John 14:27
20	Psalm 50:10-11
21	1 Thessalonians 5:17

*When I say "meditate" I do not mean incantations or lotus postures. Instead, I mean a time where you block out busy routines – prayer lists, study requirements, etc.

    a. Read the verse out loud two times.
    b. What does the verse mean to you now that you worry constantly?
    c. Do you believe the verse with your mind and your heart?
    d. How will you think differently?
    e. How will I act differently?
    f. Memorize the verse.

Everyone wants to rejoice. But that can seem like mission impossible when you worry constantly. However, meditating on the verses in Step 3 for 15 minutes per day for 21 days will give you victory over your negative statements/questions. Then, you will be able to rejoice in the Lord.

4. **Replace each negative statement/question you listed in Step 2 with a verse from today's passage from Step 3.**

For example, replace: "What if my unemployment benefits run out before I find another job?"

With: "My God shall supply all your need according to His riches in glory by Christ Jesus." (Philippians 4:19)

5. **Keep a journal.**

The Lord gave me this answer, "Write down clearly what I reveal to you." (Habakkuk 2:2)

Some things you might want to record in your journal:

  a. Your thoughts
  b. Prayers
  c. Answers you have seen to prayers
  d. Things you have learned
  e. Progress (or lack thereof) you have made

6. **Select an accountability partner.**

"Two are better than one, because they have a good reward for their labor. For if they fall, one will lift up his companion. But woe to him who is alone when he falls, for he has no one to help him up." (Ecclesiastes 4:9)

a. An accountability partner

1) Helps clarify goals. Sharing your goals with someone moves you towards achieving them.

2) Offers encouragement. A partner encourages you to keep moving towards your goals.

3) Challenges you. There may be times when you need a little "tough love". A partner reminds you of what you are working towards and how it will change your life.

b. What to look for when selecting an accountability partner.

1) Trust. Select someone that you trust. Otherwise, you will never get the full benefits of the relationship.

2) Honesty. Select someone who will be completely honest with you.

3) Confidentiality. Select someone who will keep all information discussed between the two of you, without any exceptions.

4) Non-judgmental. Select someone who understands that their role is to listen, ask questions and offer feedback, but never to judge.

5) Common Core Beliefs. Select someone who shares your beliefs. For example, if you believe it is possible to control your feelings by controlling your thinking, your accountability partner must believe the same thing.

c. Get the maximum benefit from the partnership.

1) Be clear on your goal(s).

2) Meet with your partner (face-to-face or by telephone) once per week for three weeks.

3) Make notes in your journal on progress so you can follow-up at the next meeting.

4) Keep the commitment to meet on the agreed-upon date at the agreed-upon time.

7. Draw inspiration from a man who chose to rejoice instead of worry.

Robert worried constantly. He analyzed past events, saying "If only". He also worried about the future and continually asked "what if", what if I lose my job, what if I get sick. He reached the point that he was so stressed out he did not know where to turn.

At about that time he heard a song that said we should pray instead of worry. He tried it and he was amazed that he could not worry and pray at the same time. Since then, whenever he finds himself starting to worry, he does what God's word tells us to do – "Cast all of my care upon Him, for He cares for me." (1 Peter 5:7) Although Satan tries to tempt him into worrying, Robert avoids the temptation by:

a. Spending 30 minutes reading and meditating on God's word every morning.

b. Serving others. "Serve others in love." (Galatians 5:13)

Robert discovered that whenever he worried, all of the focus was on himself. When he helps others, the focus is on them. So, he has "adopted" an elderly widow in his neighborhood. He looks in on her regularly, runs errands for her and mows her lawn. She appreciates it but Robert gets more out of it than she does. He also volunteers at a soup kitchen serving meals to the hungry.

   c. Living one day at a time. "Do not worry about tomorrow for tomorrow will worry about its own things." (Matthew 6:34)

When he took inventory of his worries, Robert discovered that most of the things he worried about were related to tomorrow. So, after beginning each day by asking God to provide everything he needs for today, he does not worry about tomorrow.

   d. Counting his blessings. "Through the Lord's mercies we are not consumed, because His compassions fail not. They are new every morning." (Lamentations 3:22-23)

Robert listed of all of his blessings and he adds to the list regularly. Whenever he is tempted to worry, he reads some of the items on the list.

   e. Meditating on the words to one of his favorite songs, *Count Your Blessings*

Count Your Blessings

When upon life's billows you are tempest tossed,
When you are discouraged thinking all is lost,
Count your many blessings, name them one by one,
And it will surprise you what the Lord hath done.

Are you ever burdened with a load of care?
Does the cross seem heavy you are called to bear?
Count your many blessings, every doubt will fly,
and you will be singing as the days go by.

So, amid the conflicts, whether great or small,
Do not be discouraged, God is over all;
Count your many blessings, angels will attend,
Help and comfort give you to your journey's end.

Summary: By changing his thinking, Robert went from worrying himself sick to thanking God for his blessings and serving others.

8. Draw inspiration from how God brought you through a previous problem.

"Remember how the LORD your God led you all the way in the wilderness these forty years, to humble and test you in order to know what was in your heart, whether or not you would keep his commands. He humbled you, causing you to hunger and then feeding you with manna, which neither you nor your ancestors had known, to teach you that man does not live on bread alone but on every word that comes from the mouth of the LORD. Your clothes did not wear out and your feet did not swell during these forty years." (Deuteronomy 8:2-4)

    a. List a problem that you had in the past.

    b. Describe how God brought you through it.

9. Guard against negative statements/questions.

"We demolish arguments and every pretension that sets itself up against the knowledge of God, and we take captive every thought to make it obedient to Christ." (2 Corinthians 10:5)

Since you have grown accustomed to making negative statements/questions to yourself which cause you to worry, you will be inclined to continue doing so. When you are tempted, ask yourself, "Is this statement/question aligned with what God says?" If not, immediately replace it with a verse from today's passage in Step 3.

Chapter Eleven

I Feel Guilty

GUILT IS defined as "a feeling of remorse for some offense or wrong." Unlike worrying, which is a preoccupation with negative thoughts about past or future negative events, guilt is focused exclusively on negative thoughts about the past. Past events cannot steal your joy. What you choose to say to yourself about past events can. Why? What you choose say to yourself determines how you feel. For example, if you tell yourself "I should not have discussed the information that was shared with me in private", you will feel down. On the other hand, if you tell yourself, "I made a mistake. I am moving on" you will be able to rejoice.

You cannot control past events. You can control what you say to yourself. In order to rejoice, you must replace the negative statements/questions that you say to yourself. These nine steps will help you accomplish that:

1. **Examine typical negative statements/questions that people say to themselves:**

    "I am accountable for past sins."
    "I have to work to earn my salvation."
    "I have trouble shaking off the old me."
    "I am suffering the effects from my sin. God must not have forgiven me."
    "I should have made different choices."

2. List negative statements/questions that you say to yourself in the left column below:

Negative statements/ questions	Replace each with a verse from today's passage in Step 3

3. Meditate* on today's passage for 15 minutes per day for the next 21 days.

"Fix these words of mine in your hearts and minds; tie them as symbols on your hands and bind them on your foreheads. Teach them to your children, talking about them when you sit at home and when you walk along the road, when you lie down and when you get up." (Deuteronomy 11:18-19)

Day	Today's Passage
1	Psalm 103:12
2	Jeremiah 31:34
3	Isaiah 1:18
4	Psalm 85:2
5	Matthew 17:20
6	Ephesians 2:8-9
7	1 John 2:12
8	Micah 7:19
9	Philippians 3:13-14
10	Psalm 118:24
11	Romans 5:9
12	1 John 1:7
13	Isaiah 43:25
14	Jeremiah 33:8
15	2 Corinthians 5:17
16	Hebrews 8:12-13
17	Titus 2:14
18	2 Chronicles 30:8-9
19	Isaiah 55:6-7
20	1 John 1:9
21	1 Thessalonians 5:17

*When I say "meditate" I do not mean incantations or lotus postures. Instead, I mean a time where you block out busy routines – prayer lists, study requirements, etc.

    a. Read the verse out loud two times.
    b. What does the verse mean to you now that you feel guilty?
    c. Do you believe the verse with your mind and your heart?
    d. How will you think differently?
    e. How will you act differently?
    f. Memorize the verse.

Everyone wants to rejoice. But that can seem like mission impossible when you feel guilty. However, meditating on the verses in Step 3 for 15 minutes per day for 21 days will give you victory over your negative statements/questions. Then, you will be able to rejoice in the Lord.

4. Replace each negative statement/question you listed in Step 2 with a verse from today's passage in Step 3.

For example, replace: "I am accountable for past sins."

With: "As far as the east is from the west, so far has He removed our transgressions from us." (Psalm 103:12)

5. Keep a journal.

The Lord gave me this answer, "Write down clearly what I reveal to you." (Habakkuk 2:2)

Some things you might want to record in your journal:

    a. Your thoughts
    b. Prayers
    c. Answers you have seen to prayers
    d. Things you have learned
    e. Progress (or lack thereof) you have made

6. Select an accountability partner.

"Two are better than one, because they have a good reward for their labor. For if they fall, one will lift up his companion. But woe to him who is alone when he falls, for he has no one to help him up." (Ecclesiastes 4:9)

a. An accountability partner

    1) Helps clarify goals. Sharing your goals with someone moves you towards achieving them.

2) Offers encouragement. A partner encourages you to keep moving towards your goals.

3) Challenges you. There may be times when you need a little "tough love". A partner reminds you of what you are working towards and how it will change your life.

b. What to look for when selecting an accountability partner.

1) Trust. Select someone that you trust. Otherwise, you will never get the full benefits of the relationship.

2) Honesty. Select someone who will be completely honest with you.

3) Confidentiality. Select someone who will keep all information discussed between the two of you, without any exceptions.

4) Non-judgmental. Select someone who understands that their role is to listen, ask questions and offer feedback, but never to judge.

5) Common Core Beliefs. Select someone who shares your beliefs. For example, if you believe it is possible to control your feelings by controlling your thinking, your accountability partner must believe the same thing.

c. Get the maximum benefit from the partnership.

1) Be clear on your goal(s).

2) Meet with your partner (face-to-face or by telephone) once per week for three weeks.

3) Make notes in your journal on progress so you can follow-up at the next meeting.

4) Keep the commitment to meet on the agreed-upon date at the agreed-upon time.

7. Draw inspiration from a woman who chose to rejoice as she overcame her guilt.

Lola met Trent in 1978. He was a good looking, kindhearted man. They began dating and having a great time. Although both of them were working, neither was making a large salary. In order to stretch their money, they decided to move in together.

This was a terrific arrangement. Pooling their resources enabled them to afford a nicer apartment than either of them could have individually. They even had money to do extra things that they had been unable to do before. They made plans for their future by returning to school for advanced degrees.

Then, Lola learned that she was pregnant. That was not something they had counted on. Both of them were in shock. Being careful about getting pregnant hadn't been good enough.

Having a child and the attached responsibilities put everything they wanted to do in jeopardy. Both of them were scared. Lola asked Trent what they should do. Since he clearly did not want to get married, he suggested an abortion.

Since that was not something she wanted to do, Lola agonized over the decision for several days. In the end, she felt that she did not have a choice.

A few days later, convinced that this was her only viable option, she scheduled the abortion. She immediately felt guilty. Trent said he wanted to be there to show his support, but she declined and went alone. So, it was done.

She never told anyone, not even her family. She simply carried on. But she still felt incredible guilt.

Two years went by. Lola completed her advanced degree and she and Trent went their separate ways. She began her career as a teacher.

A teacher from Lola's team invited her to go to church the following Sunday. Lola accepted. She enjoyed the service and meeting new people. She returned the following Sunday. During that service the pastor talked about all of us being sinners and what we needed to do to be saved.

Lola received Jesus Christ as her Savior that day that day. But she still felt guilty about her abortion.

She became a regular attendee at the church and she joined a small Bible Study group. Yet, she continued to carry her guilt.

Finally, Lola confided to Brenda, a friend from her small group, that she had had an abortion. Brenda was an absolute answer to prayer. First, she talked with Lola for over two hours about the grace of God and forgiveness in Christ, and that Lola needed to completely trust Him for it. Brenda challenged Lola by asking her, "If God can forgive you, why can you not forgive yourself?" Then she pointed out some verses for Lola to read:

a. "As far as the east is from the west, so far has He removed our transgressions from us." (Psalm 103:12)

b. "Having now been justified by His blood, we shall be saved from wrath through Him." (Romans 5:9)

c. "For I will forgive their iniquity, and their sin I will remember no more." (Jeremiah 31:34)

It was hard to let the guilty feelings go, but Lola did. She accepted God's forgiveness and forgave herself.

Summary: As a result of changing her thinking, Lola's guilt has given way to joy. She says, "I simply trust in the mercy and grace of

Christ and His wondrous forgiveness. I certainly do not deserve it, but by faith I receive it."

8. Draw inspiration from how God brought you through a previous problem.

"Remember how the LORD your God led you all the way in the wilderness these forty years, to humble and test you in order to know what was in your heart, whether or not you would keep his commands.

He humbled you, causing you to hunger and then feeding you with manna, which neither you nor your ancestors had known, to teach you that man does not live on bread alone but on every word that comes from the mouth of the LORD. Your clothes did not wear out and your feet did not swell during these forty years." (Deuteronomy 8:2-4)

List a problem that you had in the past.

Describe how God brought you through it.

9. Guard against negative statements/questions.

"We demolish arguments and every pretension that sets itself up against the knowledge of God, and we take captive every thought to make it obedient to Christ." (2 Corinthians 10:5)

Since you have grown accustomed to making negative statements/questions to yourself that cause you to feel guilty, you will be inclined to continue doing so. When you are tempted, ask yourself, "Is this statement/question aligned with what God says?" If not, immediately replace it with a verse from today's passage in Step 3.

Chapter Twelve

I Was Sexually Abused

ACCORDING TO the American Academy of Child Adolescent Psychiatry, child sexual abuse has been reported up to 80,000 times a year. Having been abused as a child cannot steal your joy. What you choose to say to yourself about being abused can. Why? What you say to yourself determines how you feel. For example, if you say to yourself, "I feel worthless because I allowed myself to be abused", you will feel down. On the other hand, if you tell yourself "I refuse to let my past dictate my future", you will be able to rejoice.

You cannot control whether you were sexually abused. You can control what you say to yourself. In order to rejoice, you must replace the negative statements/questions that you say to yourself. These nine steps will help you accomplish that:

1. **Examine typical statements/questions that people say to themselves:**

   "Why did God allow this to happen to me?"
   "I feel like my abuser got off free."
   "I will never forgive my abuser."
   "After all these years I still feel tainted."
   "I cannot trust a man."

2. **List negative statements/questions that you say to yourself in the left column below:**

Negative statements/ questions	Replace each with a verse from today's passage in Step 3

3. **Meditate* on today's passage for 15 minutes per day for the next 21 days.**

"Fix these words of mine in your hearts and minds; tie them as symbols on your hands and bind them on your foreheads. Teach them to your children, talking about them when you sit at home and when you walk along the road, when you lie down and when you get up." (Deuteronomy 11:18-19)

Day	Today's Passage
1	Psalm 34:19
2	2 Corinthians 4:17-18
3	Psalm 18:48
4	Psalm 140:12
5	Romans 8:28
6	2 Samuel 22:28
7	Psalm 103:6
8	Romans 12:19
9	Luke 6:37
10	Matthew 6:14
11	Matthew 5:44-45
12	Psalm 22:24
13	Psalm 72:14
14	Psalm 9:9
15	Psalm 118:24
16	Acts 14:22
17	Romans 8:18
18	2 Corinthians 1:3-4
19	John 10:10
20	Philippians 4:4
21	1 Thessalonians 5:17

*When I say "meditate" I do not mean incantations or lotus postures. Instead, I mean a time where you block out busy routines – prayer lists, study requirements, etc.

    a. Read the verse out loud two times.
    b. What does the verse mean to you now that you have been sexually abused?
    c. Do you believe the verse with your mind and your heart?
    d. How will you think differently?
    e. How will I act differently?

 f. Memorize the verse.

Everyone wants to rejoice. But that can seem like mission impossible when have been sexually abused. However, meditating on the verses in Step 3 for 15 minutes per day for 21 days will give you victory over your negative statements/ questions. Then, you will be able to rejoice in the Lord.

4. Replace each negative statement/question you listed in Step 2 with a verse from today's passage in Step 3.

For example, replace: "Why did God allow this to happen to me?"

With: "Many are the afflictions of the righteous, but the Lord delivers him out of them all." (Psalm 34:19)

5. Keep a journal.

The Lord gave me this answer, "Write down clearly what I reveal to you." (Habakkuk 2:2)

Some things you might want to record in your journal:

 a. Your thoughts
 b. Prayers
 c. Answers you have seen to prayers
 d. Things you have learned
 e. Progress (or lack thereof) you have made

6. Select an accountability partner.

"Two are better than one, because they have a good reward for their labor. For if they fall, one will lift up his companion. But woe to him who is alone when he falls, for he has no one to help him up." (Ecclesiastes 4:9)

a. An accountability partner

1) Helps clarify goals. Sharing your goals with someone moves you towards achieving them.

2) Offers encouragement. A partner encourages you to keep moving towards your goals.

3) Challenges you. There may be times when you need a little "tough love". A partner reminds you of what you are working towards and how it will change your life.

b. What to look for when selecting an accountability partner.

1) Trust. Select someone that you trust. Otherwise, you will never get the full benefits of the relationship.

2) Honesty. Select someone who will be completely honest with you.

3) Confidentiality. Select someone who will keep all information discussed between the two of you, without any exceptions.

4) Non-judgmental. Select someone who understands that their role is to listen, ask questions and offer feedback, but never to judge.

5) Common Core Beliefs. Select someone who shares your beliefs. For example, if you believe it is possible to control your feelings by controlling your thinking, your accountability partner must believe the same thing.

c. Get the maximum benefit from the partnership.

1) Be clear on your goal(s).

2) Meet with your partner (face-to-face or by telephone) once per week for three weeks.

3) Make notes in your journal on progress so you can follow-up at the next meeting.

4) Keep the commitment to meet on the agreed-upon date at the agreed-upon time.

7. Draw inspiration from a woman who chose to rejoice as she overcame being sexually abused.

Sandra's stepfather began molesting her when she was just seven years old. Even though she felt that it was wrong, she did not say anything. Her stepfather had told her it was their secret. Besides, he said no one would believe her if she told someone. Her stepfather was a successful businessman and their family looked completely normal from the outside.

Sandra became a Christian at the age of ten. She didn't understand why God did not stop her stepfather from touching her. She recalls asking God, "Why are you letting me suffer this way?" She considered telling her mom, but she figured her mom would not believe her or would say it was her fault.

During the next five years, the molestation became more frequent. Still, Sandra said nothing.

At 18 and having graduated from high school, she moved into an apartment with a girlfriend.

She began dating, but had a hard time trusting men.

One day her mom called and said her stepfather had been killed in an auto accident. She says, "I was very angry, and I began running around screaming, 'I hate him! I hate him!' She was furious that he would never pay for what he had done to her.

She realized that only God could help ease the painful memories, so she turned to Him for comfort. She began reading God's word and keeping a journal of her thoughts and feelings. She came to several realizations:

a. God didn't cause her to be sexually abused by her stepfather.

"We must through many tribulations enter the kingdom of God." (Acts 14:22)

b. It was important to forgive her stepfather.

"If you forgive men their trespasses, your heavenly Father will also forgive you. But if you do not forgive men their trespasses, neither will your Father forgive your trespasses." (Matthew 6:14-15)

c. She could still rejoice, despite what having been abused.

"For our light affliction, which is but for a moment, is working for us a far more exceeding and eternal weight in glory, while we do not look at the things which are seen, but the things which are unseen. For the things which are seen are temporary, but the things which are not seen are eternal." (2 Corinthians 4:17-18)

"I consider that the sufferings of this present time are not worthy to be compared with the glory which shall be revealed in us." (Romans 8:18)

Sandra began to feel a comfort deep in her heart and her soul. She knew it was God that was comforting her.

"Blessed be the God and Father of our Lord Jesus Christ, the Father of mercies and God of all comfort, who comforts us in all of tribulation, that we may be able to comfort those who are in any tribulation, with the comfort with which we ourselves are comforted by God." (2 Corinthians 1:3-4)

d. It was important to share her story in order to help others feeling similar pain.

Sandra began speaking to other abuse victims.

Summary: Today, Sandra is married to a wonderful man and has two beautiful kids. Because she changed what she tells herself, Sandra speaks to groups to help prevent others from being sexually abused. She also counsels sexual abuse victims, assuring them that they can rejoice.

8. Draw inspiration from how God brought you through a previous problem.

"Remember how the LORD your God led you all the way in the wilderness these forty years, to humble and test you in order to know what was in your heart, whether or not you would keep his commands. He humbled you, causing you to hunger and then feeding you with manna, which neither you nor your ancestors had known, to teach you that man does not live on bread alone but on every word that comes from the mouth of the LORD. Your clothes did not wear out and your feet did not swell during these forty years." (Deuteronomy 8:2-4)

a. List a problem that you had in the past.

b. Describe how God brought you through it.

9. Guard against negative statements/questions.

"We demolish arguments and every pretension that sets itself up against the knowledge of God, and we take captive every thought to make it obedient to Christ." (2 Corinthians 10:5)

Since you have grown accustomed to making negative statements/questions to yourself about having been sexually abused, you will be inclined to continue doing so. When you are tempted, ask yourself, "Is this statement/question aligned with what God says?" If not, immediately replace it with a verse from today's passage in Step 3.

Chapter Thirteen

I Am Depressed

DEPRESSION IS defined as feeling sad, blue, unhappy, miserable, or down in the dumps about your circumstances. In some cases, these feelings can interfere with everyday life for weeks or longer. Circumstances cannot make you depressed. What you choose to say to yourself about circumstances can. Why? What you say to yourself determines how you feel. For example, if you say to yourself, "I should go back and finish my degree, but I may fail" you will feel down. On the other hand, if you say to yourself, "I am going back to school and I will succeed", you will be able to rejoice.

You cannot control circumstances. You can control what you say to yourself. In order to rejoice, you must replace the negative statements/questions that you say to yourself. These nine steps will help you accomplish that:

1. Examine typical negative statements/questions that people say to themselves:

"I am so discouraged."
"I have faith but that does not help."
"I don't see any hope of things getting better."
"I should be able to beat this on my own."

2. List negative statements/questions that you say to yourself in the left column below:

Negative statements/ questions	Replace each with a verse from today's passage in Step 3

3. Meditate* on today's passage for 15 minutes per day for the next 21 days.

"Fix these words of mine in your hearts and minds; tie them as symbols on your hands and bind them on your foreheads. Teach them to your children, talking about them when you sit at home and when you walk along the road, when you lie down and when you get up." (Deuteronomy 11:18-19)

Day	Today's Passage
1	Matthew 17:20
2	Psalm 42:11
3	2 Corinthians 5:7
4	Deuteronomy 31:8
5	1 Samuel 30:6
6	Psalm 9:9
7	Proverbs 12:25
8	Deuteronomy 33:27
9	2 Samuel 22:29
10	Psalm 77:11-12
11	Psalm 143:5
12	Psalm 103:2-4
13	Nehemiah 8:10
14	James 2:20
15	Psalm 119:15-16
16	Mark 9:23
17	Romans 5:3
18	2 Corinthians 7:6
19	Philippians 4:5-7
20	James 4:10
21	1 Thessalonians 5:17

*When I say "meditate" I do not mean incantations or lotus postures. Instead, I mean a time where you block out busy routines – prayer lists, study requirements, etc.

 a. Read the verse out loud two times.
 b. What does the verse mean to you now that you are depressed?
 c. Do I believe the verse with your mind and your heart?
 d. How will you think differently?
 e. How will you act differently?
 f. Memorize the verse.

Everyone wants to rejoice. But that can seem like mission impossible when you are depressed. However, meditating on the verses in Step 3 for 15 minutes per day for 21 days will give you victory over your negative statements/questions. Then, you will be able to rejoice in the Lord.

4. Replace each negative statement/question you listed in Step 2 with a verse from today's passage in Step 3.

For example, replace: "I am so discouraged."

With: "Why are you cast down, O my soul? Why are you disquieted within me? Hope in God." (Psalm 42:11)

5. Keep a journal.

The Lord gave me this answer, "Write down clearly what I reveal to you." (Habakkuk 2:2)

Some things you might want to record in your journal:

- a. Your thoughts
- b. Prayers
- c. Answers you have seen to prayers
- d. Things you have learned
- e. Progress (or lack thereof) you have made

6. Select an accountability partner.

"Two are better than one, because they have a good reward for their labor. For if they fall, one will lift up his companion. But woe to him who is alone when he falls, for he has no one to help him up." (Ecclesiastes 4:9)

a. An accountability partner

1) Helps clarify goals. Sharing your goals with someone moves you towards achieving them.

2) Offers encouragement. A partner encourages you to keep moving towards your goals.

3) Challenges you. There may be times when you need a little "tough love." A partner reminds you of what you are working towards and how it will change your life.

b. What to look for when selecting an accountability partner.

1) Trust. Select someone that you trust. Otherwise, you will never get the full benefits of the relationship.

2) Honesty. Select someone who will be completely honest with you.

3) Confidentiality. Select someone who will keep all information discussed between the two of you, without any exceptions.

4) Non-judgmental. Select someone who understands that their role is to listen, ask questions and offer feedback, but never to judge.

5) Common Core Beliefs. Select someone who shares your beliefs. For example, if you believe it is possible to control your feelings by controlling your thinking, your accountability partner must believe the same thing.

c. Get the maximum benefit from the partnership.

1) Be clear on your goal(s).

2) Meet with your partner (face-to-face or by telephone) once per week for three weeks.

3) Make notes in your journal on progress so you can follow-up at the next meeting.

4) Keep the commitment to meet on the agreed-upon date at the agreed-upon time.

7. Draw inspiration from a woman who chose to rejoice as she overcame depression.

Kim had built her life around her husband and daughter. She lived to take care of them and did so for many years.

Even as she took care of them, she felt unfulfilled. She expected them to provide the fulfillment that she was lacking. Yet, it never came. She also felt a need to do more to further her development. However, her low self esteem kept getting in the way.

Family circumstances would eventually change.

First her husband died. So, she no longer had him to take care of. Her daughter, who was 16 at the time and very independent, told Kim that she needed to establish her own life because she would be leaving for college in a couple of years.

Kim knew she needed to get on with her life. But the thought of going back to school, getting a job outside of the home and building new relationships terrified her. Kim's friend, Will, pointed out that she had been using her late husband and daughter as crutches. Now that they no longer needed her, it was time for her move forward with her life. Will encouraged her to step out and do something. It did not matter if it was what she would wind up doing for the rest of her life, but to just get started moving in some direction. Kim gave Will all of the "Yes, but" lines, "Yes you are right, but you don't understand." All the time she was experiencing more and more sadness. On the one hand she knew that she needed to get on with her life, but on the other she was gripped by worry, fear, and doubt.

Kim wanted to go back to school. But the thought of doing it terrified her. After all, she thought, she had been out of school for more than 20 years. Besides, she had not been a particularly good student when she was in school. She thought, "What if I fail?"

Kim became more and more isolated. At one point she dropped out of sight for a week. During that time she considered ending her pain by taking her own life. Just as she was considering that possibility, a TV announcer mentioned that a local hospital was offering a seminar for people who were experiencing depression. Kim wrote down the telephone number and immediately called and registered for the seminar.

On the day of the seminar, the auditorium was filled to capacity with people suffering from depression. The speaker was a well-known former politician. He pointed out that he had battled depression for years. In fact, he said he had dropped out of politics because he had been diagnosed with clinical depression. He went on to say that, although he was no longer involved in politics, he was leading a very productive and fulfilling life.

Attending the seminar showed Kim that: 1) she was not the only person dealing with depression and, 2) she could take action to alter the course of her life.

The next week she went to a doctor, who placed her on medication for depression. While it helped, Kim did not like the way the medication made her feel. She had the doctor change to a different medicine. She did not like the way that made her feel, either.

Finally, she took herself off all medication.

Kim prayed and asked God to help her. She accepted Jesus Christ as her Lord and Savior and began attending a Bible-teaching church every Sunday. She also read and meditated on several verses from the Bible. Verses that had a large impact were:

a. "Everything is possible for him who believes." (Mark 9:23)

b. "I can do all things through Christ who strengthens me." (Philippians 4:13)

c. "If you have faith as a mustard seed, you will say to this mountain, "Move from here to there", and it will move and nothing will be impossible for you." (Matthew 17:20)

d. "Fear not, for I am with you; be not dismayed, for I am your God. I will strengthen you, yes, I will help you, I will uphold you with my righteous right hand." (Isaiah 41:10)

e. "Be anxious for nothing, but in everything by prayer and supplication with thanksgiving let your requests be made known to God; and the peace of God which surpasses all understanding, will guard your hearts and minds in Christ Jesus." (Philippians 4:6-7)

She also started a daily exercise program, watched Joyce Meyer every morning and surrounded herself with joyful, encouraging people.

She went back to school and finished at the top of her class. Later, she achieved a national certification. She took a position with a national company and is now one of their most outstanding employees.

Summary: Kim credits her remarkable turnaround to her faith in God and to her changing what she says to herself. Today, she counsels others on the importance of changing their thinking and she encourages them to be who God has called them to be and to do what God has called them to do.

8. Draw inspiration from how God brought you through a previous problem.

"Remember how the LORD your God led you all the way in the wilderness these forty years, to humble and test you in order to know what was in your heart, whether or not you would keep his commands. He humbled you, causing you to hunger and then feeding you with manna, which neither you nor your ancestors had known, to teach you that man does not live on bread alone but on every word that comes from the mouth of the LORD. Your clothes did not wear out and your feet did not swell during these forty years." (Deuteronomy 8:2-4)

a. List a problem that you had in the past.

b. Describe how God brought you through it.

9. Guard against negative statements/questions.

"We demolish arguments and every pretension that sets itself up against the knowledge of God, and we take captive every thought to make it obedient to Christ." (2 Corinthians 10:5)

Since you have grown accustomed to making negative statements/questions to yourself about being depressed, you will be inclined to continue doing so. When you are tempted, ask yourself, "Is this statement/question aligned with what God says?" If not, immediately replace it with a verse from today's passage in Step 3.

Chapter Fourteen

I Have Low Self-Esteem

SELF-ESTEEM is our overall opinion of ourselves — how we honestly feel about our abilities and limitations. Your abilities and limitations cannot steal your joy. What you choose to say to yourself about your abilities and limitations can. Why? What you say to yourself determines how you feel. For example, if you tell yourself "I don't have the ability to succeed" you will feel discouraged. On the other hand, if you tell yourself "I have the ability to achieve my goals" you will be able to rejoice.

You cannot control what caused you to develop low self esteem. You can control what you say to yourself. In order to rejoice, you must replace the negative statements/questions that you say to yourself. These nine steps will help you accomplish that:

1. **Examine typical negative statements/questions that people say to themselves:**

   "I am not very attractive."
   "I am not very competent."
   "I am not intelligent."
   "I am not very successful."
   "I am not worth much."

2. **List negative statements/questions that you say to yourself in the left column below:**

Negative statements/ questions	Replace each with a verse from today's passage in Step 3

3. **Meditate* on today's passage for 15 minutes per day for the next 21 days.**

"Fix these words of mine in your hearts and minds; tie them as symbols on your hands and bind them on your foreheads. Teach them to your children, talking about them when you sit at home and when you walk along the road, when you lie down and when you get up." (Deuteronomy 11:18-19)

Day	Today's Passage
1	Psalm 139:14
2	Psalm 119:73
3	Ephesians 2:10
4	Genesis 1:27
5	1 Corinthians 15:5
6	2 Corinthians 3:5
7	Philippians 4:13
8	2 Corinthians 9:8
9	1 Corinthians 2:4-5
10	Matthew 17:20
11	Isaiah 64:8
12	James 1:5
13	Micah 6:8
14	2 Corinthians 2:15
15	Jeremiah 29:11
16	Romans 8:37
17	Deuteronomy 28:13
18	Romans 8:16-17
19	1 Peter 2:9-10
20	John 3:16
21	1 Thessalonians 5:17

*When I say "meditate" I do not mean incantations or lotus postures. Instead, I mean a time where you block out busy routines – prayer lists, study requirements, etc.

    a. Read the verse out loud two times.
    b. What does the verse mean to you now that you have low self-esteem?
    c. Do you believe the verse with your mind and your heart?
    d. How will you think differently?
    e. How will you act differently?

f. Memorize the verse.

Everyone wants to rejoice. But that can seem like mission impossible when you have low self-esteem. However, meditating on the verses in Step 3 for 15 minutes per day for 21 days will give you victory over your negative statements/questions. Then, you will be able to rejoice in the Lord.

4. Replace each negative statement/question you listed in Step 2 with a verse from today's passage in Step 3.

For example, replace: "I am not very attractive."

With: "I will praise You, for I am fearfully and wonderfully made. Marvelous are Your works, and that my soul knows very well." (Psalm 139:14)

5. Keep a journal.

The Lord gave me this answer, "Write down clearly what I reveal to you." (Habakkuk 2:2)

Some things you might want to record in your journal:

   a. Your thoughts
   b. Prayers
   c. Answers you have seen to prayers
   d. Things you have learned
   e. Progress (or lack thereof) you have made

6. Select an accountability partner.

"Two are better than one, because they have a good reward for their labor. For if they fall, one will lift up his companion. But woe to him who is alone when he falls, for he has no one to help him up." (Ecclesiastes 4:9)

a. An accountability partner

1) Helps clarify goals. Sharing your goals with someone moves you towards achieving them.

2) Offers encouragement. A partner encourages you to keep moving towards your goals.

3) Challenges you. There may be times when you need a little "tough love". A partner reminds you of what you are working towards and how it will change your life.

b. What to look for when selecting an accountability partner.

1) Trust. Select someone that you trust. Otherwise, you will never get the full benefits of the relationship.

2) Honesty. Select someone who will be completely honest with you.

3) Confidentiality. Select someone who will keep all information discussed between the two of you, without any exceptions.

4) Non-judgmental. Select someone who understands that their role is to listen, ask questions and offer feedback, but never to judge.

5) Common Core Beliefs. Select someone who shares your beliefs. For example, if you believe it is possible to control your feelings by controlling your thinking, your accountability partner must believe the same thing.

c. Get the maximum benefit from the partnership.

1) Be clear on your goal(s).

2) Meet with your partner (face-to-face or by telephone) once per week for three weeks.

3) Make notes in your journal on progress so you can follow-up at the next meeting.

4) Keep the commitment to meet on the agreed-upon date at the agreed-upon time.

7. Draw inspiration from a man who chose to rejoice while overcoming low self-esteem.

Moses was 80 years old and had not accomplished much in his life. Much to his surprise, God selected him to lead the Israelites out of slavery in Egypt.

"Come now, therefore, and I will send you to Pharaoh that you may bring my people, the children of Israel, out of Egypt" (Exodus 3:10)

But Moses said to God, "Who am I that I should go to Pharaoh, and that I should bring the children of Israel out of Egypt?" (Exodus 3:11)

God's response: "I will certainly be with you." (Exodus 3:12)

Then Moses said to God, "Indeed, when I come to the children of Israel and say to them, "The God of your fathers has sent me to you," and they say to me, "What is His name?" What shall I say to them?" (Exodus 3:13)

And God said to Moses, "I AM WHO I AM." And He said, Thus you shall say to the children of Israel, "I AM has sent me." (Exodus 3:14)

Moses said, "But suppose they will not believe me or listen to my voice; suppose they say, "The Lord has not appeared to you." (Exodus 4: 1)

God performed several miracles to demonstrate to Moses that He, indeed, was God.

Moses said to the Lord, "O My Lord, I am not eloquent, neither before nor since You have spoken to your servant; I am slow of speech and slow of tongue." (Exodus 4:10)

God said, "Now therefore, go, I will be with your mouth and teach you what you shall say." (Exodus 4:12)

But he said, "O my Lord, please send by the hand of whomever else You may send." (Exodus 4:13)

Again, God assured Moses that He would be with him.

Ultimately, Moses followed God's command and led the children of Israel out of slavery in Egypt.

Moses and the children of Israel rejoiced. (Exodus 15:1-21)

Things we can learn from Moses' experience

    a. God has a plan for our life.

    b. In and of ourselves, we are inadequate to carry out that plan.

    c. God will go with us to carry out the plan.

    d. With God's help, we will succeed in carrying out the plan.

    e. We are to trust God, even if we don't believe in ourselves.

Summary: Moses changed his negative self-talk and relied on God's promises. He went from thinking he was not qualified to lead the children of Israel out of slavery to rejoicing when he saw God part the sea, allowing the Israelites to come through on dry land, and drown the Egyptians.

8. Draw inspiration from how God brought you through a previous problem.

"Remember how the Lord your God led you all the way in the wilderness these forty years, to humble and test you in order to know what was in your heart, whether or not you would keep his commands. He humbled you, causing you to hunger and then feeding you with manna, which neither you nor your ancestors had known, to teach you that man does not live on bread alone but on every word that comes from the mouth of the Lord. Your clothes did not wear out and your feet did not swell during these forty years." (Deuteronomy 8:2-4)

a. List a problem that you had in the past.

b. Describe how God brought you through it.

9. Guard against negative statements/questions.

"We demolish arguments and every pretension that sets itself up against the knowledge of God, and we take captive every thought to make it obedient to Christ." (2 Corinthians 10:5)

Since you have grown accustomed to making negative statements/questions to yourself about your abilities and limitations, you will be inclined to continue doing so. When you are tempted, ask yourself, "Is this statement/question aligned with what God says?" If not, immediately replace it with a verse from today's passage in Step 3.

Chapter Fifteen

I Have an Addiction

HAVING AN ADDICTION cannot steal your joy. What you choose to say to yourself about having an addiction can. Why? What you say to yourself determines how you feel. For example, if you say to yourself, "I have to drink (or drug) to drown my sorrows" you will feel discouraged. On the other hand, if you tell yourself "I will turn my will and my life over to God's care" you will be able to rejoice.

So, in order to overcome your addiction and rejoice, you must replace the negative statements/questions that you say to yourself. These nine steps will help you accomplish that:

1. **Examine typical negative statements/questions that people say to themselves:**

    "I am not hurting anybody but myself."
    "I don't have time (or money) to get help."
    "I'll handle it myself."
    "Nobody is going to tell me what to do."
    "I'd be ok if it weren't for you."

2. List negative statements/questions that you say to yourself in the left column below:

Negative statements/ questions	Replace each with a verse from today's passage in Step 3

3. Meditate* on today's passage for 15 minutes per day for the next 21 days.

"Fix these words of mine in your hearts and minds; tie them as symbols on your hands and bind them on your foreheads. Teach them to your children, talking about them when you sit at home and when you walk along the road, when you lie down and when you get up." (Deuteronomy 11:18-19)

Day	Today's Passage
1	1 Corinthians 6:19-20
2	Philippians 4:19
3	Philippians 4:13
4	Matthew 17:20
5	Galatians 5:22-23
6	1 Corinthians 6:12
7	Galatians 5:1
8	Ephesians 5:18
9	Philippians 4:8
10	James 4:10
11	1 Corinthians 10:12
12	Romans 14:12
13	2 Corinthians 12:9
14	Ecclesiastes 4:9-12
15	Matthew 7:7-8
16	1 Peter 5:8
17	1 Corinthians 15:33
18	John 8:36
19	Psalm 50:15
20	James 4:7
21	1 Thessalonians 5:17

*When I say "meditate" I do not mean incantations or lotus postures. Instead, I mean a time where you block out busy routines – prayer lists, study requirements, etc.

   a. Read the verse out loud two times.
   b. What does the verse mean to you now that you have an addiction?
   c. Do I believe the verse with my mind and my heart?
   d. How will I think differently?

e. How will I act differently?
f. Memorize the verse.

Everyone wants to rejoice. But that can seem like mission impossible when you have an addiction. However, meditating on the verses in Step 3 for 15 minutes per day for 21 days will give you victory over your negative statements/questions. Then, you will be able to rejoice in the Lord.

4. Replace each negative statement/question you listed in Step 2 with a verse from today's passage in Step 3.

For example, replace: "I am not hurting anybody but myself."

With: "Do you not know that your body is the temple of the Holy Spirit who is in you, who you have from God, and you are not your own? For you were bought at a price; therefore glorify God in your body and in your spirit, which are God's." (1 Corinthians 6:19-20)

5. Keep a journal.

The Lord gave me this answer, "Write down clearly what I reveal to you." (Habakkuk 2:2)

Some things you might want to record in your journal:

a. Your thoughts
b. Prayers
c. Answers you have seen to prayers
d. Things you have learned
e. Progress (or lack thereof) you have made

6. Select an accountability partner.

"Two are better than one, because they have a good reward for their labor. For if they fall, one will lift up his companion. But

woe to him who is alone when he falls, for he has no one to help him up." (Ecclesiastes 4:9)

a. An accountability partner

1) Helps clarify goals. Sharing your goals with someone moves you towards achieving them.

2) Offers encouragement. A partner encourages you to keep moving towards your goals.

3) Challenges you. There may be times when you need a little "tough love". A partner reminds you of what you are working towards and how it will change your life.

b. What to look for when selecting an accountability partner.

1) Trust. Select someone that you trust. Otherwise, you will never get the full benefits of the relationship.

2) Honesty. Select someone who will be completely honest with you.

3) Confidentiality. Select someone who will keep all information discussed between the two of you, without any exceptions.

4) Non-judgmental. Select someone who understands that their role is to listen, ask questions and offer feedback, but never to judge.

5) Common Core Beliefs. Select someone who shares your beliefs. For example, if you believe it is possible to control your feelings by controlling your thinking, your accountability partner must believe the same thing.

c. Get the maximum benefit from the partnership.

1) Be clear on your goal(s).

2) Meet with your partner (face-to-face or by telephone) once per week for three weeks.

3) Make notes in your journal on progress so you can follow-up at the next meeting.

4) Keep the commitment to meet on the agreed-upon date at the agreed-upon time.

7. Draw inspiration from a man who chose to rejoice while overcoming an addiction.

Sean was raised in a Southern Baptist home. From his earliest memories, he and his family attended church. He accepted Christ at a middle school church retreat.

Although drinking was not allowed in his home, he began drinking when he was 17. He drank through college. After college, he got married, got a job and had two daughters.

After the second daughter, Sean began drinking more heavily. He and his wife, Debbie, fought constantly. He blamed her for his drinking. Finally, he and Debbie got a divorce and she got custody of the children

Now that he was on his own, and feeling guilty about being such a lousy dad and ruining his marriage, he drank even more.

All the time he kept telling himself he could quit drinking any time he wanted to. This went on for approximately 10 years. During that time he was arrested three times for driving under the influence of alcohol (DUI), he was fired from a very good job and he had severe financial difficulties.

After his last DUI arrest, the judge ordered Sean to attend Alcoholics Anonymous meetings while he awaited trial. Each time a trial date was set, it got postponed. That meant more Alcohol Anonymous meetings. This turned out to be huge blessing for Sean.

He began noticing that attendees fell into two groups; the first group consistently made excuses and blamed others or their circumstances for their problems. They continued to get arrested, get DUIs, have family problems, work problems, etc. The second group admitted they were powerless over alcohol and had asked God to help them remain sober. The members of this group had been sober 10, 15, 20, 25 years, had no DUIs, no family problems, no work problems, etc.

The stark contrast in the outcomes for the two groups made a huge impact on Sean.

Finally, during a business trip, Sean got down on his knees and re-committed his life to God. He asked God to take control of his life and do whatever He chose. Sean felt as if a giant burden had been lifted from his shoulders. He was overwhelmed with peace and joy. He did not feel the urge to drink.

Through a co-worker, Sean found a Bible-teaching church and began reading his Bible regularly.

Some of his favorite verses were:

a. "Many are the afflictions of the righteous, but the Lord delivers him from them all." (Psalm 34:19)

b. "For our light affliction, which is for a moment, is working for us a far more exceeding and eternal weight in glory, while we do not look at the things which are seen. For the things which are seen are temporary, but the things which are not seen are eternal." (2 Corinthians 4:17-18)

c. "I can do all things through Christ who gives me the strength." (Philippians 4:13)

d. "But the fruit of the Spirit is love, joy, peace, forbearance, kindness, goodness, faithfulness, gentleness and self-control. Against such things there is no law." (Galatians 5:22-23)

e. "All things are lawful for me, but all things are not beneficial. All things are lawful for me, but I will not be brought under the power of anything." (1 Corinthians 6:12)

f. "Stand fast therefore in the liberty by which Christ has made us free, and do not be entangled again with a yoke of bondage." (Galatians 5:1)

g. "Do not be drunk with wine, in which is dissipation; but be filled with the Spirit." (Ephesians 5:18)

h. "Humble yourselves in the sight of the Lord, and He will lift you up." (James 4:10)

i. "When the righteous cry for help, the Lord hears and delivers them out of all their troubles." (Psalms 34:17)

Sean has not had a drink in twenty years.

In 1995, he met Debra. They hit it off right away. They got married in June 1996. Today, they have two lovely daughters. Sean has also built positive relationships with his two daughters from his previous marriages.

Summary: Sean says his twenty years of sobriety and his being alive are due to his faith in God and to replacing negative thoughts with God's word. Today, he mentors young men by sharing his experiences. He helps them achieve sobriety, and has helped many of them find a relationship with Jesus. One of his favorite expressions is "I can't, He can, I think I'll let Him."

8. Draw inspiration from how God brought you through a previous problem.

"Remember how the Lord your God led you all the way in the wilderness these forty years, to humble and test you in order to know what was in your heart, whether or not you would keep his commands. He humbled you, causing you to hunger and then feeding you with manna, which neither you nor your ancestors had known, to teach you that man does not live on bread alone but on every word that comes from the mouth of the Lord. Your clothes did not wear out and your feet did not swell during these forty years." (Deuteronomy 8:2-4)

    a. List a problem that you had in the past.

    b. Describe how God brought you through it.

9. Guard against negative statements/questions.

"We demolish arguments and every pretension that sets itself up against the knowledge of God, and we take captive every thought to make it obedient to Christ." (2 Corinthians 10:5)

Since you have grown accustomed to making negative statements/questions to yourself about having an addiction, you will be inclined to continue doing so. When you are tempted, ask yourself, "Is this statement/question aligned with what God says?" If not, immediately replace it with a verse from today's passage in Step 3.

Part Four

DEATH PROBLEMS

Chapter Sixteen

My Child Died of an Illness

ACCORDING TO the Center for Disease Control and Prevention, approximately 15,000 children age 1 – 24 die each year from cancer, heart disease or other causes. Although having a child die of any cause can be challenging, it cannot steal your joy. What you choose to say to yourself about having a child die can. Why? What you say to yourself determines how you feel. For example, if you say to yourself, "My daughter died way too young" you will be discouraged. On the other hand, if you say to yourself, "My daughter is resting in Jesus' arms and I look forward to seeing her again", you will be able to rejoice.

You cannot control whether your child dies of cancer, heart disease or some other cause. You can control what you say to yourself. In order to rejoice, you must replace the negative statements/questions that you say to yourself. These nine steps will help you accomplish that:

1. **Examine typical negative statements/questions that people say to themselves:**

   "It is horrible that my daughter died and left two small children."
   "A child is not supposed to die before his/her parents."
   "The hardest thing for a parent to do is bury a child."
   "It has been eight months but I find myself crying all the time."
   "I am angry that God has been taken away my child."

2. **List negative statements/questions that you say to yourself in the left column below:**

Negative statements/ questions	Replace each with a verse from today's passage in Step 3

3. **Meditate* on today's passage for 15 minutes per day for the next 21 days.**

"Fix these words of mine in your hearts and minds; tie them as symbols on your hands and bind them on your foreheads. Teach them to your children, talking about them when you sit at home and when you walk along the road, when you lie down and when you get up." (Deuteronomy 11:18-19)

Day	Today's Passage
1	2 Corinthians 4:17-18
2	2 Samuel 12:23
3	Psalm 118:24
4	Psalm 34:1
5	1 Corinthians 15:55
6	Luke 23:43
7	2 Corinthians 5:8
8	Psalm 30:5
9	Psalm 147:3
10	Psalm 16:11
11	John 11:25
12	1 Thessalonians 4:13
13	Revelation 21:4
14	John 11:23
15	Philippians 1:21
16	Psalm 116:15
17	Romans 14:8
18	Matthew 5:4
19	Philippians 3:20-21
20	John 14:1 – 3
21	1 Thessalonians 5:17

*When I say "meditate" I do not mean incantations or lotus postures. Instead, I mean a time where you block out busy routines – prayer lists, study requirements, etc.

    a. Read the verse out loud two times.
    b. What does the verse mean to you now that your child has died of cancer, heart disease or some other illness?
    c. Do you believe the verse with your mind and your heart?
    d. How will you think differently?
    e. How will you act differently?

f. Memorize the verse.

Everyone wants to rejoice. But that can seem like mission impossible when your child has died of cancer, heart disease or some other illness. However, meditating on the verses in Step 3 for 15 minutes per day for 21 days will give you victory over your negative statements/questions. Then, you will be able to rejoice in the Lord.

4. Replace each negative statement/question you listed in Step 2 with a verse from today's passage in Step 3.

For example, replace: "A child should not die before his parents."

With: "I shall go to him, but he shall not return to me." (2 Samuel 12:23)

5. Keep a journal.

The Lord gave me this answer, "Write down clearly what I reveal to you." (Habakkuk 2:2)

Some things you might want to record in your journal:

a. Your thoughts
b. Prayers
c. Answers you have seen to prayers
d. Things you have learned
e. Progress (or lack thereof) you have made

6. Select an accountability partner.

"Two are better than one, because they have a good reward for their labor. For if they fall, one will lift up his companion. But woe to him who is alone when he falls, for he has no one to help him up." (Ecclesiastes 4:9)

a. **An accountability partner**

1) Helps clarify goals. Sharing your goals with someone moves you towards achieving them.

2) Offers encouragement. A partner encourages you to keep moving towards your goals.

3) Challenges you. There may be times when you need a little "tough love". A partner reminds you of what you are working towards and how it will change your life.

b. **What to look for when selecting an accountability partner.**

1) Trust. Select someone that you trust. Otherwise, you will never get the full benefits of the relationship.

2) Honesty. Select someone who will be completely honest with you.

3) Confidentiality. Select someone who will keep all information discussed between the two of you, without any exceptions.

4) Non-judgmental. Select someone who understands that their role is to listen, ask questions and offer feedback, but never to judge.

5) Common Core Beliefs. Select someone who shares your beliefs. For example, if you believe it is possible to control your feelings by controlling your thinking, your accountability partner must believe the same thing.

c. **Get the maximum benefit from the partnership.**

1) Be clear on your goal(s).

2) Meet with your partner (face-to-face or by telephone) once per week for three weeks.

3) Make notes in your journal on progress so you can follow-up at the next meeting.

4) Keep the commitment to meet on the agreed-upon date at the agreed-upon time.

7. Draw inspiration from a mother who chose to rejoice despite having a child die.

Although Elizabeth Budd has watched 2 of her 3 children go and be with Jesus, she rejoices every day.

First it was Michael, who was diagnosed with AIDS in September 1991. Elizabeth served as his primary caregiver, sleeping by his bedside, whether he was at home or in the hospital. He went to be with Jesus on September 2, 1992. (See Chapter 7 – I have a Terminal Illness)

Fourteen years later, on July 11, 2006, one of Elizabeth's two daughters, Gayle, went to be with Jesus. (See Chapter 8 – I have a Chronic Illness)

Several verses have brought Elizabeth comfort and enabled her to rejoice:

a. "In everything give thanks." (1 Thessalonians 5:18)

Elizabeth thanked God for AIDS because God used it to bring Michael into a relationship with Christ.

b. "The earth is the Lord's and all its fullness, the world and those who dwell therein." (Psalm 24:1)

Many people tell Elizabeth that parents are supposed to die before children, not the other way around. She always responds by telling them that, although God allowed her to raise them, they were His children. In fact, she says, she is God's child, too. Therefore, God has the right to call His children home in whatever order He chooses.

   c. "I do not want you to be ignorant, brethren, concerning those who have fallen asleep, lest you sorrow as others who have no hope." (1 Thessalonians 4:13)

People often comment that she does not seem sad despite two of her children having died. Elizabeth says, "You might see some tears sometime, but they are tears of joy."

   d."I shall go to him, but he shall not return to me." (2 Samuel 12:23)

Elizabeth gets great joy from knowing that the children God allowed her to raise are with God and that someday she will be reunited with them in God's kingdom.

   e. "Praise is to the God and Father of our Lord Jesus Christ, the Father of compassion and the God of all comfort, who comforts us in all our troubles, so that we can comfort those in any trouble with the comfort we ourselves have received from God." (2 Corinthians 1:3-4)

Elizabeth counseled other parents who had a child living with AIDS, and in many cases, she counseled parents after the child died. Today, she serves as a model of faith for many mothers whose children have died.

   f. "Serve one another in love." (Galatians 5:13)

At 87, Elizabeth often prepares meals for neighbors and she volunteers at nursing home every month. She has some arthritis but says, "We know that if our earthly house, this tent, is destroyed, we have a building from God, a house not made with hands, eternal in the heavens." (2 Corinthians 5:1)

She frequently reflects on one of her favorite songs, *When We All Get to Heaven*

> When we all get to Heaven,
> What a day of rejoicing that will be!
> When we all see Jesus,
> We'll sing and shout the victory!

Elizabeth has already begun to shout for victory.

Summary: Elizabeth resisted all negative self-talk from the time she learned that Michael had AIDS and when she recognized that Gayle was not going to be on earth much longer. Instead, she kept her thoughts focused on God's promises. As a result, she not only rejoices, but continues to allow God to use her as a source of encouragement to others.

8. Draw inspiration from how God brought you through a previous problem.

"Remember how the LORD your God led you all the way in the wilderness these forty years, to humble and test you in order to know what was in your heart, whether or not you would keep his commands. He humbled you, causing you to hunger and then feeding you with manna, which neither you nor your ancestors had known, to teach you that man does not live on bread alone but on every word that comes from the mouth of the LORD. Your clothes did not wear out and your feet did not swell during these forty years." (Deuteronomy 8:2-4)

   a. List a problem that you had in the past.

   b. Describe how God brought you through it.

9. Guard against negative statements/questions.

"We demolish arguments and every pretension that sets itself up against the knowledge of God, and we take captive every thought to make it obedient to Christ." (2 Corinthians 10:5)

Since you have grown accustomed to making negative statements/questions to yourself about your child dying of cancer, heart disease or other illness, you will be inclined to continue doing so. When you are tempted, ask yourself, "Is this statement/question aligned with what God says?" If not, immediately replace it with a verse from today's passage in Step 3.

Chapter Seventeen

My Child Died in an Accident

ACCORDING TO the Center for Disease Control and Prevention, approximately 15,000 children age 1 – 24 die each year as a result of an accident. Although having a child die in an accident can be challenging, it cannot steal your joy. What you choose to say to yourself about having a child die in an accident can. Why? What you say to yourself determines how you you feel. For example, if you tell yourself, "I will never get over having my child die in an accident" you will feel down. On the other hand, if you tell yourself "Every day when I wake up I am one day closer to being reunited with my child" you will be able to rejoice.

You cannot control whether a child dies in an accident. You can control what you say to yourself. In order to rejoice, you must replace the negative statements/questions that you say to yourself. These nine steps will help you accomplish that:

1. **Examine typical negative statements/questions that people say to themselves:**

   "I have lost my child."
   "How could God allow this to happen?"
   "I will never forgive the person responsible for this devastation I feel."
   "How can I go on?"

"If only I had not let him go alone."

2. **List negative statements/questions that you say to yourself in the left column below:**

Negative statements/ questions	Replace each with a verse from today's passage in Step 3

3. **Meditate* on today's passage for 15 minutes per day for the next 21 days.**

"Fix these words of mine in your hearts and minds; tie them as symbols on your hands and bind them on your foreheads. Teach them to your children, talking about them when you sit at home and when you walk along the road, when you lie down and when you get up." (Deuteronomy 11:18-19)

Day	Today's Passage
1	Psalm 24:1
2	Psalm 34:19
3	2 Corinthians 4:17-18
4	Psalm 34:1
5	Matthew 6:15
6	Romans 8:28
7	Psalm 116:15
8	2 Samuel 12:23
9	Philippians 3:13-14
10	1 Thessalonians 4:14
11	John 3:16
12	Romans 6:23
13	Luke 23:43
14	1 Corinthians 15:55
15	John 11:26
16	2 Corinthians 5:6
17	Isaiah 25:8
18	1 Peter 2:24
19	2 Timothy 4:6-8
20	1 Thessalonians 5:9
21	1 Thessalonians 5:17

*When I say "meditate" I do not mean incantations or lotus postures. Instead, I mean a time where you block out busy routines – prayer lists, study requirements, etc.

    a. Read the verse out loud two times.
    b. What does the verse mean to you now that your child has died in an accident?
    c. Do you believe the verse with your mind and your heart?
    d. How will you think differently?
    e. How will you act differently?

f. Memorize the verse.

Everyone wants to rejoice. But that can seem like mission impossible when your child has died in an accident. However, meditating on the verses in Step 3 for 15 minutes per day for 21 days will give you victory over your negative statements/ questions. Then, you will be able to rejoice in the Lord.

4. Replace each negative statement/question you listed in Step 2 with a verse from today's passage in Step 3.

For example, replace: "I have lost my child."

With: The earth is the Lord's, and all its fullness, the world and those who dwell therein. (Psalm 24:1)

5. Keep a journal.

The Lord gave me this answer, "Write down clearly what I reveal to you." (Habakkuk 2:2)

Some things you might want to record in your journal:

a. Your thoughts
b. Prayers
c. Answers you have seen to prayers
d. Things you have learned
e. Progress (or lack thereof) you have made

6. Select an accountability partner.

"Two are better than one, because they have a good reward for their labor. For if they fall, one will lift up his companion. But woe to him who is alone when he falls, for he has no one to help him up." (Ecclesiastes 4:9)

a. An accountability partner

1) Helps clarify goals. Sharing your goals with someone moves you towards achieving them.

2) Offers encouragement. A partner encourages you to keep moving towards your goals.

3) Challenges you. There may be times when you need a little "tough love". A partner reminds you of what you are working towards and how it will change your life.

b. What to look for when selecting an accountability partner.

1) Trust. Select someone that you trust. Otherwise, you will never get the full benefits of the relationship.

2) Honesty. Select someone who will be completely honest with you.

3) Confidentiality. Select someone who will keep all information discussed between the two of you, without any exceptions.

4) Non-judgmental. Select someone who understands that their role is to listen, ask questions and offer feedback, but never to judge.

5) Common Core Beliefs. Select someone who shares your beliefs. For example, if you believe it is possible to control your feelings by controlling your thinking, your accountability partner must believe the same thing.

c. Get the maximum benefit from the partnership.

1) Be clear on your goal(s).

2) Meet with your partner (face-to-face or by telephone) once per week for three weeks.

3) Make notes in your journal on progress so you can follow-up at the next meeting.

4) Keep the commitment to meet on the agreed-upon date at the agreed-upon time.

7. Draw inspiration from two couples who chose to rejoice despite having a child die in an accident.

Seventeen year old Melanie was returning home from the mall when a drunk driver crossed the median and hit her car head-on. Melanie was pronounced dead at the scene.

Melanie's parents, Marlon and Sue, felt shock, then anger at the person who had done this horrible thing to their baby. But being angry did not feel right to them. After all, their pastor had just done a series of messages on forgiveness.

Marlon and Sue prayed and meditated on some of the verses their pastor had mentioned:

a. "If you forgive men when they sin against you, your heavenly Father will also forgive you. But if you do not forgive men their sins, your Father will not forgive your sins." (Matthew 6:14-15)

b. "Be kind and compassionate to one another, forgiving each other, just as in Christ God forgave you." (Ephesians 4:32)

c. "Do not repay evil with evil or insult with insult, but with blessing, because to this you were called so that you may inherit a blessing." (1 Peter 3:9)

d. "Do not say, "I'll pay you back for this wrong!" Wait for the Lord, and he will deliver you." (Proverbs 20:22)

As they prayed and mediated on these verses, peace and joy replaced their anger.

Marlon and Sue did not meet the drunk driver (Frank) until the day of his trial. He admitted he was drunk and rejected any notion of a plea deal and accepted complete responsibility for his actions.

Recognizing that Frank had not set out to kill their baby, before he was led away to begin serving his sentence, Marlon and Sue sent him a note saying, "We forgive you."

They continue to have compassion for Frank. Reflecting on Romans 8:28 "All things work together for good to those who love God, to those who are called according to His purpose," their daily prayer is for God to use this experience to bring Frank into a relationship with Jesus.

Even though Marlon and Sue feel the loss of Melanie, they look forward to being reunited with her. In the meantime, they are sustained by the knowledge that she is in Jesus' care. "Precious in the sight of the Lord is the death of his saints." (Psalm 116:15)

They also draw encouragement from Horatio Spafford's response to his daughters' death.

In November 1873 Chicago businessman Horatio Spafford, his wife Anna and their four daughters had planned to travel by ship to Europe to do missionary work. On the day they were to set sail, Spafford had a business emergency and could not leave. Not wanting to disappoint his wife Anna and daughters, he sent them on ahead. He planned to follow on another ship in a few days.

On November 22, 1873 the ship on which Anna and the girls were traveling was struck by another ship. While Anna survived and was rescued, Horatio and Anna's four daughters drowned.

Her rescuers took Anna to Cardiff, Wales, where she telegraphed her husband. Her message was brief and heartbreaking, "Saved alone. What shall I do?"

As soon as he received the telegram, Horatio left Chicago to bring his wife home. While sailing across the Atlantic Ocean, the ship's captain called Horatio to the bridge. The captain informed Horatio that they were at the approximate spot where his daughters had drowned.

That night, alone in his cabin, Horatio G. Spafford penned the words to his famous hymn, *"It Is Well with My Soul."*

When peace, like a river, attendeth my way,
When sorrows like sea billows roll;
Whatever my lot, Thou has taught me to say,
It is well, it is well, with my soul.

It is well, with my soul,
It is well, with my soul,
It is well, it is well, with my soul.

Though Satan should buffet, though trials should come,
Let this blest assurance control,
That Christ has regarded my helpless estate,
And hath shed His own blood for my soul.
(Refrain)

My sin, oh, the bliss of this glorious thought!
My sin, not in part but the whole,
Is nailed to the cross, and I bear it no more,
Praise the Lord, praise the Lord, O my soul!
(Refrain)

And Lord, haste the day when my faith shall be sight,
The clouds be rolled back as a scroll;
The trump shall resound, and the Lord shall descend,
Even so, it is well with my soul.

It is well, with my soul,
It is well, with my soul,
It is well, it is well, with my soul.

Horatio's faith in God never faltered. He later wrote Anna's half-sister, "On Thursday last we passed over the spot where she went down, in mid-ocean, the waters three miles deep. But I do not think of our dear ones there. They are safe, folded, the dear lambs."

Summary: Because of their pastor's messages on forgiveness, their willingness to keep their minds focused on God's words and Horatio Spafford's example, Marlon and Sue continue to rejoice. Resisting the negative thoughts Satan tries to send their way, they have started a scholarship in Melanie's name. They will give it to a deserving high school senior in their town annually.

8. Draw inspiration from how God brought you through a previous problem.

"Remember how the Lord your God led you all the way in the wilderness these forty years, to humble and test you in order to know what was in your heart, whether or not you would keep his commands. He humbled you, causing you to hunger and then feeding you with manna, which neither you nor your ancestors had known, to teach you that man does not live on bread alone but on every word that comes from the mouth of the Lord. Your clothes did not wear out and your feet did not swell during these forty years." (Deuteronomy 8:2-4)

List a problem that you had in the past.

Describe how God brought you through it.

9. Guard against negative statements/questions.

"We demolish arguments and every pretension that sets itself up against the knowledge of God, and we take captive every thought to make it obedient to Christ." (2 Corinthians 10:5)

Since you have grown accustomed to making negative statements/questions to yourself about your child dying in an accident, you will be inclined to continue doing so. When you are tempted, ask yourself, "Is this statement/question aligned with what God says?" If not, immediately replace it with a verse from today's passage in Step 3.

Chapter Eighteen

My Loved One Was Murdered

ACCORDING TO the Center for Disease Control and Prevention, 18,000 people were murdered in 2007. Although having a loved one murdered can be challenging, it cannot steal your joy. What you choose to say to yourself about having a loved one murdered can. Why? What you say to yourself determines how you feel. For example, if you tell yourself "This is the worst thing that could ever happen" you will feel down. On the other hand, if you tell yourself, "My loved one is in heaven" you will be able to rejoice.

You cannot control whether a loved one is murdered. You can control what you say to yourself. In order to rejoice, you must replace the negative statements/questions that you say to yourself. These nine steps will help you accomplish that:

1. **Examine typical negative statements/questions that people say to themselves:**

   "How could God allow this to happen?"
   "I cannot forgive the person who did this."
   "I am losing my faith."
   "I guess I should join a support group."
   "I feel like I could have prevented this tragedy."

2. List negative statements/questions that you say to yourself in the left column below:

Negative statements/ questions	Replace each with a verse from today's passage in Step 3

3. Meditate* on today's passage for 15 minutes per day for the next 21 days.

"Fix these words of mine in your hearts and minds; tie them as symbols on your hands and bind them on your foreheads. Teach them to your children, talking about them when you sit at home and when you walk along the road, when you lie down and when you get up." (Deuteronomy 11:18-19)

Day	Today's Passage
1	Psalm 34:1
2	1 Corinthians 16:13
3	Romans 8:28
4	Psalm 139:16
5	Luke 6:37
6	Matthew 6:14-15
7	Matthew 17:20
8	1 Thessalonians 4:13-14
9	Ecclesiastes 4:9
10	Romans 6:23
11	Luke 23:43
12	1 Corinthians 15:55
13	John 11:26
14	2 Corinthians 5:6
15	Isaiah 25:8
16	1 Peter 2:24
17	2 Timothy 4:6-8
18	John 14:1-4
19	1 Corinthians 3:21-23
20	Matthew 25:46
21	1 Thessalonians 5:17

*When I say "meditate" I do not mean incantations or lotus postures. Instead, I mean a time where you block out busy routines – prayer lists, study requirements, etc.

    a. Read the verse out loud two times.
    b. What does the verse mean to you now that your loved one has been murdered?
    c. Do you believe the verse with your mind and your heart?
    d. How will you think differently?
    e. How will you act differently?
    f. Memorize the verse.

Everyone wants to rejoice. But that can seem like mission impossible when a loved one has been murdered. However, meditating on the verses in Step 3 for 15 minutes per day for 21 days will give you victory over your negative statements/ questions. Then, you will be able to rejoice in the Lord.

4. Replace each negative statement/question you listed in Step 2 with a verse from today's passage in Step 3.

For example, replace: "How could God allow this to happen?"

With:" I will bless the Lord at all times; His praise shall continually be in my mouth." (Psalm 34:1)

5. Keep a journal.

The Lord gave me this answer, "Write down clearly what I reveal to you." (Habakkuk 2:.2)

Some things you might want to record in your journal:

   a. Your thoughts
   b. Prayers
   c. Answers you have seen to prayers
   d. Things you have learned
   e. Progress (or lack thereof) you have made

6. Select an accountability partner.

"Two are better than one, because they have a good reward for their labor. For if they fall, one will lift up his companion. But woe to him who is alone when he falls, for he has no one to help him up." (Ecclesiastes 4:9)

a. **An accountability partner**

   1) Helps clarify goals. Sharing your goals with someone moves you towards achieving them.

2) Offers encouragement. A partner encourages you to keep moving towards your goals.

3) Challenges you. There may be times when you need a little "tough love". A partner reminds you of what you are working towards and how it will change your life.

b. What to look for when selecting an accountability partner.

1) Trust. Select someone that you trust. Otherwise, you will never get the full benefits of the relationship.

2) Honesty. Select someone who will be completely honest with you.

3) Confidentiality. Select someone who will keep all information discussed between the two of you, without any exceptions.

4) Non-judgmental. Select someone who understands that their role is to listen, ask questions and offer feedback, but never to judge.

5) Common Core Beliefs. Select someone who shares your beliefs. For example, if you believe it is possible to control your feelings by controlling your thinking, your accountability partner must believe the same thing.

c. Get the maximum benefit from the partnership.

1) Be clear on your goal(s).

2) Meet with your partner (face-to-face or by telephone) once per week for three weeks.

3) Make notes in your journal on progress so you can follow-up at the next meeting.

4) Keep the commitment to meet on the agreed-upon date at the agreed-upon time.

7. Draw inspiration from a daughter who chose to rejoice despite her mother being murdered.

In August, 1995 Marion received a call that no one wants to receive. Her 85 year old mother had been murdered. She was shocked and angry at the person who had committed such a brutal crime against a defenseless, old woman. Her anger was so intense that she wanted to kill the responsible person with her own hands.

After three weeks of investigation, the police told Marion that the murder had been committed by a woman who lived in her mother's neighborhood - a woman whom Marion and her mother knew.

The woman had murdered Marion's mom to get money to buy drugs. As Marion processed all of this information, she struggled to come to grips with it.

Marion began praying and asking God to give her peace about the entire situation. She also immersed herself into God's word.

She remembered one of the verses that her mother used to recite all the time: "While we are at home in the body we are absent from the Lord." (2 Corinthians 5:6) As she meditated on the verse she imagined the joy that her mother was experiencing as a result of no longer being separated from God. She also thought of her mother's favorite song, Amazing Grace. She particularly liked the stanza:

When we've been there ten thousand years,
Bright shining as the sun,
We've no less days to sing God's praise,
Than when we first begun.

Marion also meditated on "Precious in the sight of the Lord is the death of his saints." (Psalm 116:15)

Marion began to feel an incredible peace and joy. She also decided to not only forgive the woman who had killed her mom, but to pray that God would use this horrible event to deliver her from drugs and bring her into a relationship with Jesus. She thought of Romans 8:28 and asked God to knit the horrific events into good.

Summary: Marion changed her self-talk by immersing herself in God's word. As a result, she moved from wanting to kill the person who murdered her mom to praying for her salvation. Today, Marion says "My mom was going to heaven anyway. As a result of the attacker's actions, she just went earlier than I thought she would."

8. Draw inspiration from how God brought you through a previous problem.

"Remember how the LORD your God led you all the way in the wilderness these forty years, to humble and test you in order to know what was in your heart, whether or not you would keep his commands. He humbled you, causing you to hunger and then feeding you with manna, which neither you nor your ancestors had known, to teach you that man does not live on bread alone but on every word that comes from the mouth of the LORD. Your clothes did not wear out and your feet did not swell during these forty years." (Deuteronomy 8:2-4)

List a problem that you had in the past.

Describe how God brought you through it.

9. Guard against negative statements/questions.

"We demolish arguments and every pretension that sets itself up against the knowledge of God, and we take captive every thought to make it obedient to Christ." (2 Corinthians 10:5)

Since you have grown accustomed to making negative statements/questions to yourself about your loved one being murdered, you will be inclined to continue doing so. When you are tempted, ask yourself, "Is this statement/question aligned with what God says?" If not, immediately replace it with a verse from today's passage in Step 3.

Chapter Nineteen

My Loved One Committed Suicide

ACCORDING TO the Center for Disease Control and Prevention, 34,000 people took their life in 2007. Although having a loved one take their life can be challenging, it cannot steal your joy. What you choose to say to yourself about having a loved one take their life can. Why? What you say to yourself determines how you feel. For example, if you tell yourself, "I should have seen this coming and stopped it" you will feel down. On the other hand, if you tell yourself, "My loved one made a choice, and he/she is now with God" you will be able to rejoice.

You cannot control whether a loved commits suicide. You can control what you say to yourself. In order to rejoice, you must replace the negative statements/questions that you say to yourself. These nine steps will help you accomplish that:

1. **Examine typical negative statements/questions that people say to themselves:**

   "He guaranteed himself an eternity in Hell."
   "How could I have prevented this?"
   "This is the most horrible thing that could have happened."
   "Why?"
   "I am devastated."

2. **List negative statements/questions that you say to yourself in the left column below:**

Negative statements/ questions	Replace each with a verse from today's passage in Step 3

3. **Meditate* on today's passage for 15 minutes per day for the next 21 days.**

"Fix these words of mine in your hearts and minds; tie them as symbols on your hands and bind them on your foreheads. Teach them to your children, talking about them when you sit at home and when you walk along the road, when you lie down and when you get up." (Deuteronomy 11:18-19)

Day	Today's Passage
1	Romans 8:38-39
2	John 10:28-30
3	John 5:24
4	1 Thessalonians 4:13-14
5	Psalm 139:16
6	Romans 8:28
7	Luke 23:43
8	1 Corinthians 15:55
9	John 11:26
10	John 14:1-4
11	2 Corinthians 5:6
12	Isaiah 25:8
13	2 Timothy 4:6-8
14	1 Thessalonians 5:9
15	1 Corinthians 3:21-23
16	Matthew 25:46
17	1 Peter 2:24
18	1 Peter 5:6-7
19	Philippians 4:8
20	Philippians 4:4
21	1 Thessalonians 5:17

*When I say "meditate" I do not mean incantations or lotus postures. Instead, I mean a time where you block out busy routines – prayer lists, study requirements, etc.

    a. Read the verse out loud two times.
    b. What does the verse mean to you now that your loved one has committed suicide?
    c. Do I believe the verse with your mind and your heart?
    d. How will I think differently?
    e. How will I act differently?
    f. Memorize the verse.

Everyone wants to rejoice. But that can seem like mission impossible when a loved one has committed suicide. However, meditating on the verses in Step 3 for 15 minutes per day for 21 days will give you victory over your negative statements/ questions. Then, you will be able to rejoice in the Lord.

4. Replace each negative statement/question you listed in Step 2 with a verse from today's passage from Step 3.

For example, replace: "He guaranteed himself an eternity in Hell."

With: "For I am persuaded that neither death nor life, nor angels nor principalities nor powers, nor things present nor things to come, nor height nor death, nor any other created thing, shall be able to separate us from the love of God which is in Christ Jesus our Lord." (Romans 8:38-39)

5. Keep a journal.

The Lord gave me this answer, "Write down clearly what I reveal to you." (Habakkuk 2:2)

Some things you might want to record in your journal:

    a. Your thoughts
    b. Prayers
    c. Answers you have seen to prayers
    d. Things you have learned
    e. Progress (or lack thereof) you have made

6. Select an accountability partner.

"Two are better than one, because they have a good reward for their labor. For if they fall, one will lift up his companion. But woe to him who is alone when he falls, for he has no one to help him up." (Ecclesiastes 4:9)

a. **An accountability partner**

1) Helps clarify goals. Sharing your goals with someone moves you towards achieving them.

2) Offers encouragement. A partner encourages you to keep moving towards your goals.

3) Challenges. There may be times when you need a little "tough love". A partner reminds you of what you are working towards and how it will change your life.

b. **What to look for when selecting an accountability partner.**

1) Trust. Select someone that you trust. Otherwise, you will never get the full benefits of the relationship.

2) Honesty. Select someone who will be completely honest with you.

3) Confidentiality. Select someone who will keep all information discussed between the two of you, without any exceptions.

4) Non-judgmental. Select someone who understands that their role is to listen, ask questions and offer feedback, but never to judge.

5) Common Core Beliefs. Select someone who shares your beliefs. For example, if you believe it is possible to control your feelings by controlling your thinking, your accountability partner must believe the same thing.

c. **Get the maximum benefit from the partnership.**

1) Be clear on your goal(s).

2) Meet with your partner (face-to-face or by telephone) once per week for three weeks.

3) Make notes in your journal on progress so you can follow-up at the next meeting.

4) Keep the commitment to meet on the agreed-upon date at the agreed-upon time.

7. Draw encouragement from a couple who chose to rejoice despite having their teenage son commit suicide.

Debbie and Roger's middle son, Jeremy, committed suicide at age 17. Though saddened, Debbie and Roger resisted the urge to become distraught. They said, "Our faith will sustain us."

They had known that Jeremy had been struggling in some areas, but they never considered that he would take his own life. They recognized that while this had come as a shock to them, it was not a shock to God. They reflected on Psalm 139:16: "Your eyes saw my unformed body; all the days ordained for me were written in your book before one of them came to be."

Even though they were shocked and saddened, their hope was on the future as they meditated on several verses:

a. "I do not want you to be ignorant, brothers, those who have fallen asleep, lest you sorrow as others who have no hope." (1 Thessalonians 4:13)

b. "For God so loved the world that He gave his only begotten Son, that whoever believes in Him should not perish, but have everlasting life." (John 3:16)

c. "For I am persuaded, that neither death, nor life, nor angels, nor principalities, nor powers, nor things present, nor things to come, nor height, nor depth, nor any other creature, shall be able to separate us from the love of God, which is in Christ Jesus our Lord." (Romans 8:38-39)

d. Jesus said to him, "Assuredly, I say to you, today you will be with Me in Paradise." (Luke 23:43)

Following through on Jeremy's desire to help others, Debbie and Roger donated Jeremy's corneas to a local eye bank.

Summary: "Our faith will sustain us."This was Roger's comment after Jeremy's funeral service. Roger went on to say they rejoice in knowing that Jeremy is with the Lord they very much look forward to being reunited with him in heaven.

8. Draw inspiration from how God brought you through a previous problem.

"Remember how the LORD your God led you all the way in the wilderness these forty years, to humble and test you in order to know what was in your heart, whether or not you would keep his commands. He humbled you, causing you to hunger and then feeding you with manna, which neither you nor your ancestors had known, to teach you that man does not live on bread alone but on every word that comes from the mouth of the LORD. Your clothes did not wear out and your feet did not swell during these forty years." (Deuteronomy 8:2-4)

a. List a problem that you had in the past.

b. Describe how God brought you through it.

9. Guard against negative statements/questions.

"We demolish arguments and every pretension that sets itself up against the knowledge of God, and we take captive every thought to make it obedient to Christ." (2 Corinthians 10:5)

Since you have grown accustomed to making negative statements/questions to yourself about your loved one having committed suicide, you will be inclined to continue doing so. When you are tempted, ask yourself, "Is this statement/question aligned with what God says?" If not, immediately replace it with a verse from today's passage in Step 3.

Part Five

FINANCIAL PROBLEMS

Chapter Twenty

I Have Financial Problems

FINANCIAL PROBLEMS CAN be challenging, but they cannot steal your joy. What you choose to say to yourself about financial problems can. Why? What you say to yourself determines how you feel. For example, if you say to yourself "There is no way out of this hole", you will feel discouraged. On the other hand, if you say to yourself, "I will move beyond the current situation" you will be able to rejoice.

You cannot magically clear up your financial problems. You can control what you say to yourself. In order to rejoice, you must replace the negative statements/questions that you say to yourself. These nine steps will help you accomplish that:

1. **Examine typical negative statements/questions that people say to themselves:**

    "I have insufficient income."
    "My mortgage company is threatening to foreclose."
    "I have a lot of debt."
    "If only I had made better decisions."
    "Should I file for bankruptcy?"

2. List negative statements/questions that you say to yourself in the left column below:

Negative statements/ questions	Replace each with a verse from today's passage in Step 3

3. Meditate* on today's passage for 15 minutes per day for the next 21 days.

"Fix these words of mine in your hearts and minds; tie them as symbols on your hands and bind them on your foreheads. Teach them to your children, talking about them when you sit at home and when you walk along the road, when you lie down and when you get up." (Deuteronomy 11:18-19)

Day	Today's Passage
1	Psalm 37:25
2	Matthew 6:31-32
3	Philippians 4:19
4	Proverbs 12:15
5	Matthew 6:34
6	Proverbs 3:5-6
7	1 John 5:14-15
8	Matthew 7:7-8
9	Isaiah 43:2
10	John 14:14
11	Philippians 3:13
12	Psalm 121:1-2
13	Psalm 55:22
14	Jeremiah 29:11
15	Romans 8:18
16	Philippians 4:11
17	1 Peter 5:7
18	1 Thessalonians 5:17,18
19	Isaiah 41:10
20	2 Chronicles 20:15
21	Psalm 118:25

*When I say "meditate" I do not mean incantations or lotus postures. Instead, I mean a time where you block out busy routines – prayer lists, study requirements, etc.

a. Read the verse out loud two times.
b. What does the verse mean to you now that you have financial problems?
c. Do you believe the verse with your mind and my heart?
d. How will you think differently?
e. How will I act differently?
f. Memorize the verse.

Everyone wants to rejoice. But that can seem like mission impossible when you have financial challenges. However, meditating on the verses in Step 3 for 15 minutes per day for 21 days will give you victory over your negative statements/ questions. Then, you will be able to rejoice in the Lord.

4. Replace each negative statement/question you listed in Step 2 with a verse from today's passage in Step 3.

For example, replace: "How will I meet my expenses?"

With: "I have been young, and now am old; yet, I have not seen the righteous forsaken, nor His descendants begging bread." (Psalm 37:25)

5. Keep a journal.

The Lord gave me this answer, "Write down clearly what I reveal to you." (Habakkuk 2:2)

Some things you might want to record in your journal:

  a. Your thoughts
  b. Prayers
  c. Answers you have seen to prayers
  d. Things you have learned
  e. Progress (or lack thereof)

6. Select an accountability partner.

"Two are better than one, because they have a good reward for their labor. For if they fall, one will lift up his companion. But woe to him who is alone when he falls, for he has no one to help him up." (Ecclesiastes 4:9)

a. An accountability partner

1) Helps clarify goals. Sharing your goals with someone moves you towards achieving them.

2) Offers encouragement. A partner encourages you to keep moving towards your goals.

3) Challenges you. There may be times when you need a little "tough love". A partner reminds you of what you are working towards and how it will change your life.

b. What to look for when selecting an accountability partner.

1) Trust. Select someone that you trust. Otherwise, you will never get the full benefits of the relationship.

2) Honesty. Select someone who will be completely honest with you.

3) Confidentiality. Select someone who will keep all information discussed between the two of you, without any exceptions.

4) Non-judgmental. Select someone who understands that their role is to listen, ask questions and offer feedback, but never to judge.

5) Common Core Beliefs. Select someone who shares your beliefs. For example, if you believe it is possible to control your feelings by controlling your thinking, your accountability partner must believe the same thing.

c. Get the maximum benefit from the partnership.

1) Be clear on your goal(s).

2) Meet with your partner (face-to-face or by telephone) once per week for three weeks.

3) Make notes in your journal on progress so you can follow-up at the next meeting.

4) Keep the commitment to meet on the agreed-upon date at the agreed-upon time.

7. Draw inspiration from a man who chose to rejoice despite financial problems.

At 37, Harold appeared to be in great financial shape. He had a terrific job as an analyst with the federal government. He had a nice house, three cars, some rental property and a promising investment portfolio.

Since he did not have many material things as a youngster, Harold had decided that things were going to be different now. He did not deny himself any material pleasure.

He also worked long hours and went to school at night to get a master's degree in management. Since he was doing all of this, he was never at home. Needless to say, his family life suffered.

Then, everything fell apart. First, his wife found out that he was having an affair and filed for divorce. Because she was considered the more stable parent, she was awarded custody of the kids, along with a huge financial settlement. This, along with a great deal of credit card debt and some poor investment decisions, took a financial toll on Harold.

With his mortgage company threatening to foreclose on his house, things looked so bleak that Harold was considering filing bankruptcy and even taking his own life.

One day while in the grocery store Harold ran into Reggie, a former college football teammate. He had heard that Harold had hit some turbulence. He invited Harold over to his house for dinner. Harold accepted.

Harold marveled at the relationship among Reggie, his wife and kids. As Harold and Reggie talked later, Reggie mentioned that Jesus had changed his life dramatically. He invited Reggie to attend church with him and his family the following Sunday. Although, Harold had not been to church in years, he accepted. After church, Reggie invited Harold back to his house for dinner again.

Back at the house, Reggie told Harold that what he really needed was Jesus. Harold said he had messed up so much that not even Jesus could help him. Reggie assured him that he was wrong.

Harold went to church with Reggie and his family again a couple of weeks later. When the pastor had altar call, Harold went down and received Jesus Christ as his Lord and Savior.

Harold says, "As I accepted the fact that Jesus loved me so much that he died for me, I realized I had never felt this kind of joy before." He went on to say that even though he does not have all the possessions he used to have, he is more joyful than he has ever been. In fact, he says what he thought were blessings from God were actually things that had convinced him that he did not need God in his life.

Summary: As a result of changing his self-talk, Harold is no longer driven to accumulate assets. He says his mission is to use the life God has given him to bring glory to His name. He started by apologizing to his ex-wife and children for the pain he had caused them. Now, he has positive relationship with them. Acting on Biblical financial counseling to which Reggie directed him, Reggie is current on his mortgage payments and he is on his way to being debt-free.

8. Draw inspiration from how God brought you through a previous problem.

"Remember how the LORD your God led you all the way in the wilderness these forty years, to humble and test you in order to know what was in your heart, whether or not you would keep his commands. He humbled you, causing you to hunger and then feeding you with manna, which neither you nor your ancestors had known, to teach you that man does not live on bread alone but on every word that comes from the mouth of the LORD. Your clothes did not wear out and your feet did not swell during these forty years." (Deuteronomy 8:2-4)

    a. List a problem that you had in the past.

    b. Describe how God brought you through it.

9. Guard against negative statements/questions.

"We demolish arguments and every pretension that sets itself up against the knowledge of God, and we take captive every thought to make it obedient to Christ." (2 Corinthians 10:5)

Since you have grown accustomed to making negative statements/questions to yourself about having financial challenges, you will be inclined to continue doing so. When you are tempted, ask yourself, "Is this statement/question aligned with what God says?" If not, immediately replace it with a verse from today's passage in Step 3.

Part Six

FAMILY PROBLEMS

Chapter Twenty-One

I Have a Special Needs Child

ALTHOUGH HAVING A SPECIAL needs child can affect your family's life, having a special needs child cannot steal your joy. What you choose to say to yourself about having a special needs child can. Why? What you choose to say to yourself determines how you feel. For example, if you tell yourself, "God must be punishing me by giving me a special needs child" you will feel down. On the other hand, if you tell yourself, "God has a special plan for this child and He has included me in that plan", you will be able to rejoice.

You cannot control whether you have a special needs child. You can control what you say to yourself. In order to rejoice, you must replace the negative statements/questions that you say to yourself. These nine steps will help you accomplish that:

1. **Examine typical negative statements/questions that parents say to themselves:**

   "Why would God give me a special needs child?"
   "What did I do to cause God to give me a special needs child?"
   "This can't be happening to me, my child, my family."
   "What is going to happen when the child is 5 years old, 12, 21?"
   "How am I going to manage having a special needs child?"

2. **List negative statements/questions that you say to yourself:**

Negative statements/ questions	Replace each with a verse from today's passage in Step 3

3. **Meditate* on today's passage for 15 minutes per day for the next 21 days.**

"Fix these words of mine in your hearts and minds; tie them as symbols on your hands and bind them on your foreheads. Teach them to your children, talking about them when you sit at home and when you walk along the road, when you lie down and when you get up." (Deuteronomy 11:18-19)

Day	Today's Passage
1	Jeremiah 29:11
2	Ephesians 2:10
3	Psalm 34:19
4	2 Corinthians 12:9
5	Isaiah 35:5-6
6	John 9:2-3
7	Exodus 4:11
8	Matthew 19:14
9	Psalm 118:24
10	Deuteronomy 28:4
11	1 Corinthians 1:27
12	Psalm 34:1
13	Acts 20:35
14	Luke 7:22
15	Luke 14:13
16	Isaiah 40:29
17	Isaiah 42:16
18	Job 29:15
19	Matthew 6:34
20	1 Thessalonians 5:17
21	Philippians 4:19

*When I say "meditate" I do not mean incantations or lotus postures. Instead, I mean a time where you block out busy routines – prayer lists, study requirements, etc.

    a. Read the verse out loud two times.
    b. What does the verse mean to me now that you have a special needs child?
    c. Do you believe the verse with your mind and your heart?
    d. How will you think differently?
    e. How will you act differently?
    f. Memorize the verse.

Everyone wants to rejoice. But that can seem like mission impossible when you have a special needs child. However, meditating on the verses in Step 3 for 15 minutes per day for 21 days will give you victory over your negative statements/ questions. Then, you will be able to rejoice in the Lord.

4. Replace each negative statement/question you listed in Step 2 with a verse from today's passage in Step 3.

For example, replace: "What did I do to cause God to give me a special needs child?"

With: "Blessed shall be fruit of your body." (Deuteronomy 28:4)

5. Keep a journal.

The Lord gave me this answer, "Write down clearly what I reveal to you." (Habakkuk 2:2)

Some things you might want to record in your journal:

  a. Your thoughts
  b. Prayers
  c. Answers you have seen to prayers
  d. Things you have learned
  e. Progress (or lack thereof) you have made

6. Select an accountability partner.

"Two are better than one, because they have a good reward for their labor. For if they fall, one will lift up his companion. But woe to him who is alone when he falls, for he has no one to help him up." (Ecclesiastes 4:9)

a. An accountability partner

  1) Helps clarify goals. Sharing your goals with someone moves you towards achieving them.

2) Offers encouragement. A partner encourages you to keep moving towards your goals.

3) Challenges you. There may be times when you need a little "tough love". A partner reminds you of what you are working towards and how it will change your life.

b. What to look for when selecting an accountability partner.

1) Trust. Select someone that you trust. Otherwise, you will never get the full benefits of the relationship.

2) Honesty. Select someone who will be completely honest with you.

3) Confidentiality. Select someone who will keep all information discussed between the two of you, without any exceptions.

4) Non-judgmental. Select someone who understands that their role is to listen, ask questions and offer feedback, but never to judge.

5) Common Core Beliefs. Select someone who shares your beliefs. For example, if you believe it is possible to control your feelings by controlling your thinking, your accountability partner must believe the same thing.

c. Get the maximum benefit from the partnership.

1) Be clear on your goal(s).

2) Meet with your partner (face-to-face or by telephone) once per week for three weeks.

3) Make notes in your journal on progress so you can follow-up at the next meeting.

4) Keep the commitment to meet on the agreed-upon date at the agreed-upon time.

7. Draw inspiration from parents who chose to rejoice despite having a special needs child.

Elaine and Tom desperately wanted to have a baby. They prayed and trusted God to give them one when the time was right.

After having been married for two years, Elaine became pregnant. She and Tom were very excited. They made plans to turn the extra bedroom into a nursery and discussed how they were going to raise their new bundle of joy. Whenever people asked them whether they wanted a girl or boy, they said it did not matter as long as it was a healthy baby.

Early in her pregnancy, an abnormality showed up on the sonogram. Further tests revealed that their son had Down syndrome.

The doctor asked Elaine and Tom repeatedly if they wanted to continue the pregnancy.

They considered an abortion briefly, before concluding that they wanted to continue the pregnancy.

However, privately, Elaine asked herself several questions:

"Where is God?" "Why has God given us a special needs child?" "Did I do something to cause this?" "Will I be a good mother?" "Will Tom think less of me because I gave him a defective baby?" "How will we manage?" "What will happen to him when he is 8 and 12 and 16 and 25 years of age?" "Suppose we decide to have more children. Will they have special needs?"

As she asked these questions, Elaine drew comfort from several verses:

"Be strong and of good courage, do not fear nor be afraid of them; for the Lord your God, He is the One who goes with you. He will not leave you nor forsake you." (Deuteronomy 31:6)

"I know the plans I have for you, declares the Lord, plans for welfare and not for evil, to give you a future and a hope." (Jeremiah 29:11)

His disciples asked him, "Rabbi, who sinned, this man or his parents, that he was born blind?" "Neither this man nor his parents sinned," said Jesus, "but this happened so that the works of God might be displayed in him." (John 9:2-3)

Baby Luke was born on June 12, 2009.

Elaine and Tom took one look at him and felt a kind of peace and joy that amazed even them.

Elaine said, "God's giving Luke to us changed our hearts, just by being born."

Summary: Elaine went from questioning why God would give her a special needs child and worrying about the condition of future children she may have, to completely trusting God. She said, "When I think of having additional children, I no longer say as long as they are healthy. I now say, we trust God because He is in control and He will be with us and supply every need we have and bless us in ways we cannot imagine."

8. Draw inspiration from how God brought you through a previous problem.

"Remember how the Lord your God led you all the way in the wilderness these forty years, to humble and test you in order to know what was in your heart, whether or not you would keep his commands. He humbled you, causing you to hunger and then feeding you with manna, which neither you nor your ancestors had known, to teach you that man does not live on bread alone but on every word that comes from the mouth of the Lord. Your clothes did not wear out and your feet did not swell during these forty years." (Deuteronomy 8:2-4)

   a. List a problem that you had in the past.

   b. Describe how God brought you through it.

9. Guard against negative statements/questions.

"We demolish arguments and every pretension that sets itself up against the knowledge of God, and we take captive every thought to make it obedient to Christ." (2 Corinthians 10:5)

Since you have grown accustomed to making negative statements/questions to yourself about having a special needs child, you will be inclined to continue doing so. When you are tempted, ask yourself, "Is this statement/question aligned with what God says?" If not, immediately replace it with a verse from today's passage in Step 3.

Chapter Twenty-Two

I Have a Rebellious Teen

REBELLIOUS TEENS APPEAR in families regardless of financial class, ethnicity or family size. Although having a rebellious teen can be challenging, it cannot steal your joy. What you choose to say to yourself about having a having a rebellious teen can. Why? What you say to yourself determines how you feel. For example, if you say to yourself, "I have failed as a parent", you will feel down. On the other hand, if you say to yourself, "This is not my fault, and we will get through it' you will be able to rejoice.

You cannot control whether your teen rebels. You can control what you say to yourself. In order to rejoice, you must replace the negative statements/questions that you say to yourself. These nine steps will help you accomplish that:

1. **Examine typical negative statements/questions that parents say to themselves:**

   "I never acted this way when I was a teenager."
   "I feel like I have lost my son (or daughter) forever."
   "Why do I have to deal with this when no other parents seem to have this problem?"
   "I have tried several different approaches and none have worked."
   "I have poor parenting skills."

2. List negative statements/questions that you say to yourself in the left column below:

Negative statements/ questions	Replace each with a verse from today's passage in Step 3

3. Meditate* on today's passage for 15 minutes per day for the next 21 days.

"Fix these words of mine in your hearts and minds; tie them as symbols on your hands and bind them on your foreheads. Teach them to your children, talking about them when you sit at home and when you walk along the road, when you lie down and when you get up." (Deuteronomy 11:18-19)

Day	Today's Passage
1	James 1:5
2	Jeremiah 31:16-17
3	Proverbs 3:5-6
4	Joshua 1:9
5	Psalm 34:19
6	Isaiah 43:5-6
7	Psalm 119:49-50
8	1 Thessalonians 5:17
9	Isaiah 40:31
10	Lamentations 3:22-23
11	Matthew 11:28
12	2 Corinthians 4:17-18
13	Luke 1:37
14	Luke 19:10
15	Luke 15:24
16	Philippians 4:6-7
17	1 Peter 5:7
18	Romans 8:28
19	Romans 8:38
20	Jeremiah 29:11
21	2 Chronicles 20:15

*When I say "meditate" I do not mean incantations or lotus postures. Instead, I mean a time where you block out busy routines – prayer lists, study requirements, etc.

    a. Read the verse out loud two times.
    b. What does the verse mean to you now that I have a rebellious teen?
    c. Do you believe the verse with your mind and your heart?
    d. How will I think differently?
    e. How will I act differently?

    f. Memorize the verse.

Everyone wants to rejoice. But that can seem like mission impossible when you have a rebellious teen. However, meditating on the verses in Step 3 for 15 minutes per day for 21 days will give you victory over your negative statements/ questions. Then, you will be able to rejoice in the Lord.

4. Replace each negative statement/question you listed in Step 2 with a verse from today's passage in Step 3.

For example, replace: "I know no idea how to handle this situation."

With: "If any of you lacks wisdom, let him ask of God, who gives to all liberally and without reproach, and it will be given to him." (James 1:5)

5. Keep a journal.

The Lord gave me this answer, "Write down clearly what I reveal to you." (Habakkuk 2:2)

Some things you might want to record in your journal:

    a. Your thoughts
    b. Prayers
    c. Answers you have seen to prayers
    d. Things you have learned
    e. Progress (or lack thereof)

6. Select an accountability partner.

"Two are better than one, because they have a good reward for their labor. For if they fall, one will lift up his companion. But woe to him who is alone when he falls, for he has no one to help him up." (Ecclesiastes 4:9)

a. An accountability partner

1) Helps clarify goals. Sharing your goals with someone moves you towards achieving them.

2) Offers encouragement. A partner encourages you to keep moving towards your goals.

3) Challenges you. There may be times when you need a little "tough love". A partner reminds you of what you are working towards and how it will change your life.

b. What to look for when selecting an accountability partner.

1) Trust. Select someone that you trust. Otherwise, you will never get the full benefits of the relationship.

2) Honesty. Select someone who will be completely honest with you.

3) Confidentiality. Select someone who will keep all information discussed between the two of you, without any exceptions.

4) Non-judgmental. Select someone who understands that their role is to listen, ask questions and offer feedback, but never to judge.

5) Common Core Beliefs. Select someone who shares your beliefs. For example, if you believe it is possible to control your feelings by controlling your thinking, your accountability partner must believe the same thing.

c. Get the maximum benefit from the partnership.

1) Be clear on your goal(s).

2) Meet with your partner (face-to-face or by telephone) once per week for three weeks.

3) Make notes in your journal on progress so you can follow-up at the next meeting.

4) Keep the commitment to meet on the agreed-upon date at the agreed-upon time.

7. Draw inspiration from two couples who chose to rejoice despite having a rebellious teen.

Ken and Diane's story

At 15, Rich began being a behavior problem at home and at school. His grades declined dramatically. When we asked him what was going on, he said everything was okay.

The behavior problems intensified when he was 16. We learned that he was drinking and smoking marijuana. He was disrespectful and he caused all kinds of problems within the family. Since Rich dominated the family time, we did not pay much attention to our two other kids.

Diane and I had huge arguments about how to handle the situation. I was embarrassed since I was an elder at our church. We felt like we had failed as parents. We never did anything as a couple because we always felt like we should be doing something to get Rich straightened out.

We tried several approaches, but nothing worked. We thought this can't be happening to our family. In the meantime we kept wondering if Rich would ever turn around.

Finally, we realized that things were not getting better and that we had to do something drastic. We read "If any of you lacks wisdom, let him ask God, who gives to all liberally and without reproach, and it will be given to him. (James 1:5) So we asked God.

A friend at another church, whom I had confided in about our struggles with Rich, suggested that we may want to consider a residential treatment program for Rich.

After much prayer, we decided to send Rich to a Christian residential treatment program. He objected, but we stood our ground and sent him anyway.

We also joined a support group for parents of rebellious teens at another church in our community. We learned from, supported and prayed for each other.

Although we attended family counseling sessions at the treatment center, we allowed the experts to do what they do best.

In the meantime, things were very peaceful at home, for a change. We focused on our other kids. We did fun things as a family. Diane and I had a getaway weekend for the first time since our honeymoon.

We prayed. "Pray without ceasing." (1 Thessalonians 5:17)

We focused on God's word. Many verses helped us recapture the joy we had had before Rich began to rebel:

a. "I sought the Lord, and He answered me; He delivered me from all my fears." (Psalm 34:4)

b. "Those who wait on the Lord will renew their strength; they shall mount up with wings like eagles, they will run and not be weary, they will walk and not faint." (Isaiah 40:31)

c. "Come to Me, all you who labor and are heavy laden, and I will give you rest." (Matthew 11:28)

d. "With God nothing will be impossible." (Luke 1:37)

e. "Humble yourselves under the mighty hand of God, that He may exalt you in due time, casting all your care upon Him, for He cares for you." (1 Peter 5:6-7)

f. "All things God works for the good to those who love God, to those who are called according to His purpose." (Romans 8:28)

g. "I know the plans I have for you, declares the Lord. Plans to prosper you and not harm you, plans to give you a hope and a future." (Jeremiah 29:11)

h. "The battle is not yours, but God's." (2 Chronicles 20:15)

i. Two are better than one, because they have a good reward for their labor. For if they fall, one will lift up his companion. But woe to him who is alone when he falls, for he has no one to help him up." ("Ecclesiastes 4:9-10)

Thanks to all the wonderful people at the treatment center, Rich returned home a very different young man. He no longer drinks, smokes or uses drugs. He now has a deep love for God. He has learned that God cares about him and what he does. He respects himself and others.

He is maintaining a B average in all of his classes and he is a leader with the high school ministry.

He is beginning to look at colleges.

We feel like we have witnessed Luke 15:24 being played out right before our eyes.

"For this son of mine was dead and is alive again; he was lost and now is found." (Luke 15:24)

Summary: When they changed their self-talk and focused on God's word, Ken and Diane discovered that they did not have to go it alone. They further realized that God was not only with them, but that He had a plan. Now they are a resource for other parents of rebellious teens.

Fair and John Brocards' teenage son, Bubba, had become completely unmanageable. He was a constant source of tension and disruption in the household. After much prayer and discussion, Fair and John painfully decided to have Bubba removed from their home and taken to a wilderness therapy program for adolescents. After eight weeks Bubba returned home a transformed individual. The experience transformed Fair and John's lives, as well. They felt God calling them to do something to help other parents going through circumstances similar to what they had experienced.

In 2004, they founded Prodigal Child Ministries. Their mission is to provide biblical and secular support and resources for the parents of struggling teens and young adults in crisis, in order to give them hope and a future.

8. Draw inspiration from how God brought you through a previous problem.

"Remember how the LORD your God led you all the way in the wilderness these forty years, to humble and test you in order to know what was in your heart, whether or not you would keep his commands. He humbled you, causing you to hunger and then feeding you with manna, which neither you nor your ancestors had known, to teach you that man does not live on bread alone but on every word that comes from the mouth of the LORD. Your clothes did not wear out and your feet did not swell during these forty years." (Deuteronomy 8:2-4)

a. List a problem that you had in the past.

b. Describe how God brought you through it.

9. Guard against negative statements/questions.

"We demolish arguments and every pretension that sets itself up against the knowledge of God, and we take captive every thought to make it obedient to Christ." (2 Corinthians 10:5)

Since you have grown accustomed to making negative statements/ questions to yourself about having a rebellious teen, you will be inclined to continue doing so. When you are tempted, ask yourself, "Is this statement/question aligned with what God says?" If not, immediately replace it with a verse from today's passage in Step 3.

Chapter Twenty-Three

I Have a Family Conflict

CONFLICT CAN HAPPEN when family members have different points of view or beliefs. Although a family conflict can be challenging, it cannot steal your joy. What you choose to say to yourself about having a family conflict can. Why? What you say to yourself determines how you feel. For example, if you say to yourself, "If he would only listen to me things would be better" you will feel down. On the other hand, if you say to yourself, "even though I disagree with the way she does things, I value our relationship and will do everything I can to remain on good terms" you will be able to rejoice.

You may not be able to control whether you have a family conflict. You can control what you say to yourself. In order to rejoice, you must replace the negative statements/questions that you say to yourself. These nine steps will help you accomplish that:

1. **Examine the typical negative statements/questions that people say to themselves:**

   "I have told several people about the conflict I am having."
   "I can't ever forgive her for the pain she has caused me."
   "I have forgiven her before."
   "I promise I will get even with her for this."
   "She has always been that way."

2. **List negative statements/questions that you say to yourself in the left column below:**

Negative statements/ questions	Replace each with a verse from today's passage in Step 3

3. **Meditate* on today's passage for 15 minutes per day for the next 21 days.**

"Fix these words of mine in your hearts and minds; tie them as symbols on your hands and bind them on your foreheads. Teach them to your children, talking about them when you sit at home and when you walk along the road, when you lie down and when you get up." (Deuteronomy 11:18-19)

Day	Today's Passage
1	Matthew 18:15
2	Colossians 3:13
3	Matthew 6:14-15
4	Ephesians 4:32
5	Matthew 18:21-22
6	Matthew 5:7
7	Leviticus 19:18
8	Romans 12:16-18
9	James 1:19
10	Psalm 133:1
11	Romans 14:19
12	1 Thessalonians 5:11
13	Galatians 6:2
14	Philippians 2:3-4
15	Isaiah 43:18
16	Philippians 3:13-14
17	Proverbs 15:28
18	1 Thessalonians 5:17
19	1 Corinthians 4:17-18
20	James 3:17-18
21	Proverbs 12:18

*When I say "meditate" I do not mean incantations or lotus postures. Instead, I mean a time where you block out busy routines – prayer lists, study requirements, etc.

    a. Read the verse out loud two times.
    b. What does the verse mean to you now that you are involved in a family conflict?
    c. Do I believe the verse with my mind and my heart?
    d. How will you think differently?
    e. How will I act differently?
    f. Memorize the verse.

Everyone wants to rejoice. But that can seem like mission impossible when you are involved in a family conflict. However, meditating on the verses in Step 3 for 15 minutes per day for 21 days will give you victory over your negative statements/ questions. Then, you will be able to rejoice in the Lord.

4. **Replace each negative statement/question you listed in Step 2 with a verse from today's passage in Step 3.**

For example, replace: "I have told several people about the conflict I am having."

With: "If your brother sins against you go and tell him his fault between you and him alone. If he hears you, you have gained a brother." (Matthew 18:15)

5. **Keep a journal.**

The Lord gave me this answer, "Write down clearly what I reveal to you." (Habakkuk 2:2)

Some things you might want to record in your journal:

a. Your thoughts
b. Prayers
c. Answers you have seen to prayers
d. Things you have learned
e. Progress (or lack thereof)

6. **Select an accountability partner.**

"Two are better than one, because they have a good reward for their labor. For if they fall, one will lift up his companion. But woe to him who is alone when he falls, for he has no one to help him up." (Ecclesiastes 4:9)

a. An accountability partner

1) Helps clarify goals. Sharing your goals with someone moves you towards achieving them.

2) Offers encouragement. A partner encourages you to keep moving towards your goals.

3) Challenges you. There may be times when you need a little "tough love". A partner reminds you of what you are working towards and how it will change your life.

b. What to look for when selecting an accountability partner.

1) Trust. Select someone that you trust. Otherwise, you will never get the full benefits of the relationship.

2) Honesty. Select someone who will be completely honest with you.

3) Confidentiality. Select someone who will keep all information discussed between the two of you, without any exceptions.

4) Non-judgmental. Select someone who understands that their role is to listen, ask questions and offer feedback, but never to judge.

5) Common Core Beliefs. Select someone who shares your beliefs. For example, if you believe it is possible to control your feelings by controlling your thinking, your accountability partner must believe the same thing.

c. Get the maximum benefit from the partnership.

1) Be clear on your goal(s).

2) Meet with your partner (face-to-face or by telephone) once per week for three weeks.

3) Make notes in your journal on progress so you can follow-up at the next meeting.

4) Keep the commitment to meet on the agreed-upon date at the agreed-upon time.

7. Draw inspiration from a woman who chose to rejoice while working through a family conflict and a health crisis at the same time.

Evelyn's story of reconciliation with her mom.

Although I loved and respected my mother, we began clashing when I was a teenager. This continued through college and after I was married and had two children. My father, a quiet, hard-working man, had tried to keep the peace between my mother and me. But it was to no avail.

Finally, my mom and I had a bitter argument. We stopped talking. Despite my dad's attempts to bring us back together, I did not speak to my mother for almost two years. I also did not let my children visit her.

Those two years represented a horrible time —a time of not only disrespecting and falling away from my mom but from God, as well.

Then my sister told me that mom was having some health problems. My anger immediately melted away.

It turned out that my mom had cancer. She would need a double mastectomy and chemotherapy and radiation. I felt guilty for not having spoken to her for so long. I cried out to God, "What if my mom dies?" I thought "I'm too late." "I'm a terrible person and I'm being punished."

Then I remembered the verse "In all things, give thanks." (1 Thessalonians 5:18) I found myself thanking God for cancer. It had my mom and me back together.

I took my mom for her chemotherapy and radiation sessions. When she felt up to it, we would stop and have lunch. We talked and we prayed together.

We read scripture. I asked her to forgive me, which she did. She also asked me to forgive her, which I had already done. Mom explained that her mother had not been there for her and, as a result, she had made several mistakes. Mom had not wanted me to repeat the mistakes she had made as a teen and young adult. So, in her zest to be the perfect mom, she had gone overboard.

I realized I had disobeyed God by not honoring my mom. Instead, I had allowed my pride to get in the way. We discussed several verses, including:

   a. "Do not give the devil a foothold." (Ephesians 4:27)

   b. "Submit yourselves, then, to God. Resist the devil, and he will flee from you." (James 4:7)

   c. "Bear with one another." (Colossians 3:13)

There was such peace and joy every time we were together or talked on the telephone. Jesus had taken all my selfish anger, which had caused so many years of pain, and had changed my heart.

He changed my mom's hearts as well. During the course of her chemotherapy, she accepted Jesus as her Lord and Savior.

Mom was pronounced cancer free. Today, we have a better relationship than ever.

Now I fully believe "For with God nothing will be impossible." (Luke 1:37)

Summary: Evelyn went from being angry at her mom, to feeling guilty, to forgiving her mom, to being afraid her mom was going to die, to thanking God for the cancer. She recognized that God had used it to bring her back into a right relationship with Him and with her mom. Evelyn says the change in her thinking made it all possible.

8. Draw inspiration from how God brought you through a previous problem.

"Remember how the LORD your God led you all the way in the wilderness these forty years, to humble and test you in order to know what was in your heart, whether or not you would keep his commands. He humbled you, causing you to hunger and then feeding you with manna, which neither you nor your ancestors had known, to teach you that man does not live on bread alone but on every word that comes from the mouth of the LORD. Your clothes did not wear out and your feet did not swell during these forty years." (Deuteronomy 8:2-4)

List a problem that you had in the past.

Describe how God brought you through it.

9. Guard against negative statements/questions.

"We demolish arguments and every pretension that sets itself up against the knowledge of God, and we take captive every thought to make it obedient to Christ." (2 Corinthians 10:5)

Since you have grown accustomed to making negative statements/questions to yourself about being involved in a family conflict, you will be inclined to continue doing so. When you are tempted, ask yourself, "Is this statement/question aligned with what God says?" If not, immediately replace it with a verse from today's passage in Step 3.

Chapter Twenty Four

I Am a Caregiver/ Advocate for Aging Parents/Family Member

ACCORDING TO the Opinion Research Corporation, 22 percent of the population -- approximately 46 million Americans -- is providing care/advocating for an aging parent or other adult relative. Although being a caregiver/advocate presents many challenges, it cannot steal your joy. What you choose to say to yourself about being a caregiver/advocate can. Why? What you say to yourself determines how you feel. For example, if you say to yourself "Who signed me up for this?" you will feel down. On the other hand, if you say to yourself, "With God's help, I am committed to doing the very best I can" you will be able to rejoice.

You may not be able to control whether you are a caregiver/ advocate. You can control what you say to yourself. In order to rejoice, you must replace the negative statements/questions that you say to yourself. These nine steps will help you accomplish that:

1. **Examine typical negative statements/questions that family caregiver/advocates say to themselves:**

   "I resent having to be a caregiver."
   "I am physically and emotionally spent."
   "I can't do this alone."
   "There are other things I would rather be doing."
   "I do not feel appreciated."

2. **List negative statements/questions that you say to yourself in the left column below:**

Negative statements/ questions	Replace each with a verse from today's passage in Step 3

3. **Meditate* on today's passage for 15 minutes per day for the next 21 days.**

"Fix these words of mine in your hearts and minds; tie them as symbols on your hands and bind them on your foreheads. Teach them to your children, talking about them when you sit at home and when you walk along the road, when you lie down and when you get up." (Deuteronomy 11:18-19)

Day	Today's Passage
1	Mark 10:45
2	Exodus 20:12
3	Psalm 34:19
4	Matthew 11:28
5	1 John 3:17
6	Galatians 6:10
7	Matthew 5:16
8	Galatians 6:2
9	Ecclesiastes 4:9
10	1 Chronicles 28:20
11	Hebrews 6:10-12
12	Luke 10:30-35
13	Matthew 25:35-40
14	Colossians 3:23-24
15	Deuteronomy 31:6
16	2 Corinthians 5:20
17	Psalm 118:24
18	Matthew 6:34
19	Psalm 121:1-2
20	Philippians 4:11
21	1 Thessalonians 5:17

*When I say "meditate" I do not mean incantations or lotus postures. Instead, I mean a time where you block out busy routines – prayer lists, study requirements, etc.

   a. Read the verse out loud two times.
   b. What does the verse mean to you now that you are a caregiver?
   c. Do you believe the verse with your mind and my heart?
   d. How will you think differently?
   e. How will you act differently?
   f. Memorize the verse.

Everyone wants to rejoice. But that can seem like mission impossible when you are a caregiver for a family member. However, meditating on the verses in Step 3 for 15 minutes per day for 21 days will give you victory over your negative statements/questions. Then, you will be able to rejoice in the Lord.

4. **Replace each negative statement/question you listed in Step 2 with a verse from today's passage in Step 3.**

For example, replace: "I resent having to be a caregiver/ advocate."

With: "Whoever has this world's goods, and sees his brother in need, and shuts up his heart from him, how does the love of God abide in him?" (1 John 3:17)

5. **Keep a journal.**

The Lord gave me this answer, "Write down clearly what I reveal to you." (Habakkuk 2:2)

Some things you might want to record in your journal:

a. Your thoughts
b. Prayers
c. Answers you have seen to prayers
d. Things you have learned
e. Progress (or lack thereof)

6. **Select an accountability partner.**

"Two are better than one, because they have a good reward for their labor. For if they fall, one will lift up his companion. But woe to him who is alone when he falls, for he has no one to help him up." (Ecclesiastes 4:9)

a. An accountability partner

1) Helps clarify goals. Sharing your goals with someone moves you towards achieving them.

2) Offers encouragement. A partner encourages you to keep moving towards your goals.

3) Challenges you. There may be times when you need a little "tough love". A partner reminds you of what you are working towards and how it will change your life.

b. What to look for when selecting an accountability partner.

1) Trust. Select someone that you trust. Otherwise, you will never get the full benefits of the relationship.

2) Honesty. Select someone who will be completely honest with you.

3) Confidentiality. Select someone who will keep all information discussed between the two of you, without any exceptions.

4) Non-judgmental. Select someone who understands that their role is to listen, ask questions and offer feedback, but never to judge.

5) Common Core Beliefs. Select someone who shares your beliefs. For example, if you believe it is possible to control your feelings by controlling your thinking, your accountability partner must believe the same thing.

c. Get the maximum benefit from the partnership.

1) Be clear on your goal(s).

2) Meet with your partner (face-to-face or by telephone) once per week for three weeks.

3) Make notes in your journal on progress so you can follow-up at the next meeting.

4) Keep the commitment to meet on the agreed-upon date at the agreed-upon time.

7. Draw inspiration from a man who chose to rejoice while being his wife's caregiver.

I was laid off from my job in March, 1994. That coincided with my late wife, Gayle's, health beginning to deteriorate rapidly. For the next 12 years, I would be her caregiver.

Gayle had been diagnosed with crohn's disease in 1976. Her doctor had hoped to avoid treating the disease with prednisone because of the long term side effects. However, prednisone was the only drug that kept the crohn's disease under control.

So, by March 1994, as her doctor had predicted, the side effects had mounted. They included hypertension, diabetes, suppressed immune system, peripheral artery disease, glaucoma, cataracts and asthmatic bronchitis.

I did the grocery shopping, cooking, laundry. In addition, I was an advocate for Gayle in dealing with health care providers. I also became adept at providing wound care, administering intravenous antibiotics and many other nursing functions.

Several of God's truths enabled me to rejoice while being a primary caregiver for 12 years:

a. "A joyful heart is good medicine, but a broken spirit dries up the bones." (Proverbs 17:22)

We laughed every day. We laughed at movies we watched, jokes I told Gayle, things that we had experienced while in high school,

things that family members had done or said and things we had
seen as I had pushed her wheelchair through the neighborhood.

b. "Our light affliction, which is but for a moment, is working
   for us a far more exceeding and eternal weight in glory,
   while we do not look at the things which are seen, but at
   the things which are not seen. For the things which are
   seen are temporary, but the things which are not seen are
   eternal." (2 Corinthians 4:17-18)

c. "He will not leave you nor forsake you." (Deuteronomy
   31:6)

I could feel God's presence in the midst of the most mundane
tasks.

d. "God will supply all your need according to His riches in
   Christ Jesus." (Philippians 4:19)

God provided many folks to help me. For example, Gayle's
mother, Elizabeth Budd, came and stayed with us for weeks
at a time. She cooked mouth-watering meals, did laundry and
provided a steady dose of prayer and encouragement. Gayle's
aunt, Martina Beckett, assumed additional duties at home so
Elizabeth could come. In addition to bringing food, Gayle's
sister, Bessie Strand, came and stayed so I could get a good
night's sleep if I had a speaking engagement the next day.
Bessie's husband, Preston, assumed additional duties at home
so Bessie could come and help me carry Gayle for acupuncture
treatments.

Members from our church, Grace Community Church, prayed
for us regularly throughout Gayle's illness. They also visited
us at the hospital, brought meals, mowed the lawn, helped with
transportation to medical appointments, brought movies and sat
with Gayle so I could run errands or just take a brief respite.
Many people consistently went above and beyond anything we
could have expected. They included Pastor Mark Norman and
his wife, Luana, Pastor Tim Siemens and his wife, Stephanie,

Nancy and Joe Hancock, Katie and Robert Judge, Diane and Jeff Dombeck, Kathleen Grieve and Larry Monahan, Leslie and Milroy Stevenson and Winifred Cooper.

Pastor Billy R. Hunter, his wife, Cristen, and members of Gayle's home church, Bethel AME, in Onancock, VA, prayed regularly and sent encouraging cards. The church members came to visit us at the hotel during Gayle's last visit to her hometown in December, 2005. Robert Lee Chandler drove Elizabeth to visit us more times than I can remember. Oliver and Helen Chandler also drove Elizabeth to spend time with us.

e. "Let your light shine before men, that they may see your good works, and glorify your Father in heaven." (Matthew 5:16)

Gayle's chronic infections led to numerous hospitalizations, once for 48 days. The hospital staff commented on our faith and how I took such good care of Gayle.

f. "Do not worry about tomorrow, for tomorrow will worry about its own things." (Matthew 6:34)

We took one day at a time, or as Gayle said, "Sometimes, we take one minute at a time."

g. We sang a song from our childhood:

Turn your eyes upon Jesus,
Look full in His Wonderful face,
And the things of the world will grow strangely dim,
In the light of His glory and grace!

Summary: Each time Satan sent negative thoughts my way, I replaced them with verses from God's Word. As a result, I rejoiced every day, including the day God called Gayle home.

8. Draw inspiration from how God brought you through a previous problem.

"Remember how the LORD your God led you all the way in the wilderness these forty years, to humble and test you in order to know what was in your heart, whether or not you would keep his commands. He humbled you, causing you to hunger and then feeding you with manna, which neither you nor your ancestors had known, to teach you that man does not live on bread alone but on every word that comes from the mouth of the LORD. Your clothes did not wear out and your feet did not swell during these forty years." (Deuteronomy 8:2-4)

a. List a problem that you had in the past.

b. Describe how God brought you through it.

9. Guard against negative statements/questions.

"We demolish arguments and every pretension that sets itself up against the knowledge of God, and we take captive every thought to make it obedient to Christ. (2 Corinthians 10:5)

Since you have grown accustomed to making negative statements/questions to yourself about being a caregiver, you will be inclined to continue doing so. When you are tempted, ask yourself, "Is this statement/question aligned with what God says?" If not, immediately replace it with a verse from today's passage in Step 3.

Chapter Twenty-Five

I Have Marital Problems

MARITAL PROBLEMS CAN occur between any couple. Although these problems can be challenging, they cannot steal your joy. What you choose to say to yourself about having marital problems can. Why? What you say to yourself determines how you feel. For example, if you say to yourself, "I think my marriage is over", you will feel down. On the other hand, if you say to yourself "I believe we can work through our issues" you will be able to rejoice.

You may not be able to control whether you have marital problems. You can control what you say to yourself. In order to rejoice, you must replace the negative statements/questions that you say to yourself. These nine steps will help you accomplish that:

1. **Examine typical negative statements/questions that people say to themselves:**

   "This situation is ridiculous."
   "I have to use a harsh tone to get my spouse's attention."
   "I can't be completely honest with my spouse."
   "I think it is best that I clam up when I have an issue with my spouse."
   "I don't have to listen; I know what he/she is going to say."

2. List negative statements/questions that you say to yourself in the left column below:

Negative statements/ questions	Replace each with a verse from today's passage in Step 3

3. Meditate* on today's passage for 15 minutes per day for the next 21 days.

"Fix these words of mine in your hearts and minds; tie them as symbols on your hands and bind them on your foreheads. Teach them to your children, talking about them when you sit at home and when you walk along the road, when you lie down and when you get up." (Deuteronomy 11:18-19)

Day	Today's Passage
1	James 3:13-17
2	Proverbs 15:18
3	2 Corinthians 4:17-18
4	Proverbs 12:18
5	Ephesians 4:26
6	Colossians 4:6
7	Proverbs 17:27
8	Ephesians 4:15
9	Ecclesiastes 7:9
10	Isaiah 66:18
11	1 Corinthians 2:11
12	Proverbs 18:13
13	James 1:19-20
14	Proverbs 17:14
15	John 14:14
16	Proverbs 3:5-6
17	Romans 12:16
18	Philippians 2:3
19	Proverbs 16:24
20	1 Thessalonians 5:17
21	James 5:16

*When I say "meditate" I do not mean incantations or lotus postures. Instead, I mean a time where you block out busy routines – prayer lists, study requirements, etc.

    a. Read the verse out loud two times.
    b. What does the verse mean to you now that you have marital issues?
    c. Do I believe the verse with your mind and your heart?
    d. How will you think differently?
    e. How will you act differently?

    f. Memorize the verse.

Everyone wants to rejoice. But that can seem like mission impossible when you are having marital issues. However, meditating on the verses in Step 3 for 15 minutes per day for 21 days will give you victory over your negative statements/ questions. Then, you will be able to rejoice in the Lord.

4. Replace each negative statement/question you listed in Step 2 with a verse from today's passage in Step 3.

For example, replace: "This is a very unpleasant situation."

With: "For our light affliction, which is but for a moment, is working for us a far more exceeding and eternal weight in glory, while we do not look at the things which are seen, but at the things which are not seen. For the things which are seen are temporary, but the things which are not seen are eternal." (2 Corinthians 4:17-18)

5. Keep a journal.

The Lord gave me this answer, "Write down clearly what I reveal to you." (Habakkuk 2:2)

Some things you might want to record in your journal:

    a. Your thoughts
    b. Prayers
    c. Answers you have seen to prayers
    d. Things you have learned
    e. Progress (or lack thereof)

6. Select an accountability partner.

"Two are better than one, because they have a good reward for their labor. For if they fall, one will lift up his companion. But

woe to him who is alone when he falls, for he has no one to help him up." (Ecclesiastes 4:9)

a. An accountability partner

1) Helps clarify goals. Sharing your goals with someone moves you towards achieving them.

2) Offers encouragement. A partner encourages you to keep moving towards your goals.

3) Challenges you. There may be times when you need a little "tough love". A partner reminds you of what you are working towards and how it will change your life.

b. What to look for when selecting an accountability partner.

1) Trust. Select someone that you trust. Otherwise, you will never get the full benefits of the relationship.

2) Honesty. Select someone who will be completely honest with you.

3) Confidentiality. Select someone who will keep all information discussed between the two of you, without any exceptions.

4) Non-judgmental. Select someone who understands that their role is to listen, ask questions and offer feedback, but never to judge.

5) Common Core Beliefs. Select someone who shares your beliefs. For example, if you believe it is possible to control your feelings by controlling your thinking, your accountability partner must believe the same thing.

c. Get the maximum benefit from the partnership.

1) Be clear on your goal(s).

2) Meet with your partner (face-to-face or by telephone) once per week for three weeks.

3) Make notes in your journal on progress so you can follow-up at the next meeting.

4) Keep the commitment to meet on the agreed-upon   date at the agreed-upon time.

7.   Draw inspiration from a couple who chose to rejoice while working through some marital issues.

Bill and Sarah met at Starbucks. Since they were both alone, they struck up a conversation as they enjoyed their coffee. They talked so easily that they decided to have dinner the next evening. After dating for 18 months, they were married.

Although they never discussed it, each of them knew what they expected from a spouse. It only took a few months for each of them to realize that they were not getting what they had expected. So, like many couples, each of them set out to "fix" the other one.

As typically, happens, that did not go over well. So, Bill and Sarah began to argue frequently. They also began pursuing other interests – Sarah hanging out with girlfriends and Bill working later and later, and then going out for a beer with co-workers.

After 5 years, Bill had had enough and said he wanted a divorce. Sarah thought that might not be a bad idea. However, after some discussion, they decided to do a trial separation first. Bill moved out and rented a small apartment downtown near his office.

Bill still came over to pick up his mail and to mow the lawn. One day while visiting the house, Al, a neighbor invited Bill and Sarah to attend church with him and his wife, Jean, the following Sunday. Bill asked Sarah and she agreed.

During the service the pastor talked about having a relationship with Jesus. Neither Bill nor Sarah knew what he was talking about. So, they asked Al and Jean if they could explain. Al and Jean delightedly explained that we are all sinners because of Adam and Eve but that Jesus came and died for our sins. They further explained that, if we put our trust in Him, we will spend an eternity in heaven with Him.

Bill accepted Christ immediately. One of the first things he did was get down on his knees and tell Sarah how much he loved her and he apologized for the things he had done. Sarah apologized for trying to do an extreme makeover on him. Two months later Sarah accepted Christ.

Bill and Sarah reconciled and Bill moved back into the house. As new believers, they were full of joy and excitement. But they had lots of questions about how God could help them continue to build a solid marriage. Since they recognized that they couldn't do it on their own, they asked Al and Jean for their help. Al and Jean were eager to do it and they became Bill and Sarah's marriage mentors. Later, they began an in home bible study.

Some of the verses that impacted Bill and Sarah as they sought to build a new, Christ-centered relationship were:

a. "A soft answer turns away wrath, but a harsh word stirs up anger." (Proverbs 15:1)

b. "Pleasant words are like a honeycomb, sweetness to the soul and health to the bones." (Proverbs 16:24)

c. "You must regard your spouse as more important than yourself." (Philippians 2:3)

d. "Do not let the sun go down on your wrath, nor give place to the devil." (Ephesians 4:26)

e. "But let everyone be quick to hear, slow to speak and slow to anger." (James 1:19)

f. "Lean not on your own understanding; in all your ways acknowledge Him, and He shall make your path straight." (Proverbs 3:5-6)

g. "Be of the same mind toward one another. Do not be wise in your own opinion." (Romans 12:16)

h. "Confess your trespasses to one another, and pray for one another." (James 5:16)

i. "With all lowliness and gentleness, with longsuffering, bearing with one another in love." (Ephesians 4:2)

Summary: Even as they are worked to build a Christ-centered relationship, Bill and Sarah experienced incredible joy. They say God has given them a renewed love in their relationship and that He has mended every wound. They also say they are committed to continually replacing negative statements/questions with God's word.

8. Draw inspiration from how God brought you through a previous problem.

"Remember how the LORD your God led you all the way in the wilderness these forty years, to humble and test you in order to know what was in your heart, whether or not you would keep his commands. He humbled you, causing you to hunger and then feeding you with manna, which neither you nor your ancestors had known, to teach you that man does not live on bread alone but on every word that comes from the mouth of the LORD. Your clothes did not wear out and your feet did not swell during these forty years." (Deuteronomy 8:2-4)

a. List a problem that you had in the past.

b. Describe how God brought you through it.

9. Guard against negative statements/questions.

"We demolish arguments and every pretension that sets itself up against the knowledge of God, and we take captive every thought to make it obedient to Christ." (2 Corinthians 10:5)

Since you have grown accustomed to making negative statements/questions to yourself about having marital issues, you will be inclined to continue doing so. When you are tempted, ask yourself, "Is this statement/question aligned with what God says?" If not, immediately replace it with a verse from today's passage in Step 3.

Chapter Twenty-Six

I Am Heading for Divorce/Going through a Divorce/ Divorced

RESEARCHERS SAY 41 percent of all marriages ends in divorce. Although going through a divorce can be challenging, it cannot steal your joy. What you choose to say to yourself about going through a divorce can. Why? What you say to yourself determines how you feel. For example, if you say to yourself, "This is a nightmare from which I will never recover" you will feel down. On the other hand, if you say to yourself, "Even though I would rather have stayed married, I will be fine after this is over" you will be able to rejoice.

You may not be able to control whether you go through a divorce. You can control what you say to yourself. In order to rejoice, you must replace the negative statements/questions that you say to yourself. These nine steps will help you accomplish that:

1. **Examine typical negative statements/questions that people say to themselves:**

   "I can't ever forgive."

"I failed at marriage."
"I am worried about how I will manage financially."
"I have no idea how to proceed."
"I am angry."

2. **List negative statements/questions that you say to yourself in the left column below:**

Negative statements/ questions	Replace each with a verse from today's passage in Step 3

3. **Meditate* on today's passage for 15 minutes per day for the next 21 days.**

"Fix these words of mine in your hearts and minds; tie them as symbols on your hands and bind them on your foreheads. Teach them to your children, talking about them when you sit at home and when you walk along the road, when you lie down and when you get up." (Deuteronomy 11:18-19)

Day	Today's Passage
1	Mark 11:25-26
2	1 Thessalonians 5:17
3	Philippians 1:6
4	2 Corinthians 4:17-18
5	Romans 8:28
6	Psalm 118:24
7	Nehemiah 8:10
8	Proverbs 3:5-6
9	Philippians 4:19
10	Acts 14:22
11	John 16:33
12	Psalm 34:19
13	Psalm 37:8
14	Matthew 6:31-34
15	Matthew 5:7
16	James 1:5
17	Proverbs 12:18
18	Colossians 3:8
19	Leviticus 19:18
20	Ephesians 4:32
21	1 Peter 3:8-9

*When I say "meditate" I do not mean incantations or lotus postures. Instead, I mean a time where you block out busy routines – prayer lists, study requirements, etc.

- a. Read the verse out loud two times.
- b. What does the verse mean to you now that you are about to go through a divorce, going through a divorce or have recently gone through a divorce?
- c. Do you believe the verse with your mind and your heart?
- d. How will you think differently?

e. How will I act differently?

f. Memorize the verse.

Everyone wants to rejoice. But that can seem like mission impossible when you are about to go through a divorce, going through a divorce, or recently gone through a divorce. However, meditating on the verses in Step 3 for 15 minutes per day for 21 days will give you victory over your negative statements/ questions. Then, you will be able to rejoice in the Lord.

4. Replace each negative statement/question you listed in Step 2 with a verse from today's passage in Step 3.

For example, replace: "I can't ever forgive."

With: "If you have anything against anyone, forgive him, that your Father in heaven may forgive your trespasses. But if you do not forgive, neither will your father in heaven forgive your trespasses." (Mark 11:25-26).

5. Keep a journal.

The Lord gave me this answer, "Write down clearly what I reveal to you." (Habakkuk 2:2)

Some things you might want to record in your journal:

a. Your thoughts

b. Prayers

c. Answers you have seen to prayers

d. Things you have learned

e. Progress (or lack thereof) you have made

6. Select an accountability partner.

"Two are better than one, because they have a good reward for their labor. For if they fall, one will lift up his companion. But woe to him who is alone when he falls, for he has no one to help him up." (Ecclesiastes 4:9)

a. An accountability partner

1) Helps clarify goals. Sharing your goals with someone moves you towards achieving them.

2) Offers encouragement. A partner encourages you to keep moving towards your goals.

3) Challenges you. There may be times when you need a little "tough love". A partner reminds you of what you are working towards and how it will change your life.

b. What to look for when selecting an accountability partner.

1) Trust. Select someone that you trust. Otherwise, you will never get the full benefits of the relationship.

2) Honesty. Select someone who will be completely honest with you.

3) Confidentiality. Select someone who will keep all information discussed between the two of you, without any exceptions.

4) Non-judgmental. Select someone who understands that their role is to listen, ask questions and offer feedback, but never to judge.

5) Common Core Beliefs. Select someone who shares your beliefs. For example, if you believe it is possible to control your feelings by controlling your thinking, your accountability partner must believe the same thing.

c. Get the maximum benefit from the partnership.

1) Be clear on your goal(s).

2) Meet with your partner (face-to-face or by telephone) once per week for three weeks.

3) Make notes in your journal on progress so you can follow-up at the next meeting.

4) Keep the commitment to meet on the agreed-upon date at the agreed-upon time.

7. Draw inspiration from two women who chose to rejoice despite going through a divorce.

Kelly had pictured herself being married from the time she was a little girl. This image persisted throughout middle and high school. While in college, she met and fell in love with Jim. Kelly was a committed Christian and was very active in Campus Crusade for Christ. Jim was neither.

They got married shortly after graduation.

Things went great initially. Then, Kelly and Jim began having problems. Although they tried to resolve the issues, the relationship continued to deteriorate.

They sought out a counselor and even did a trial separation, thinking that would give them a chance to work out their issues.

None of it worked, however. So, after 6 years of marriage, Jim decided that the only solution was to get a divorce.

Kelly had never dreamed that they would wind up getting a divorce. However, she reluctantly agreed to the divorce. She knew she would need to rely on her faith to get going through this unpleasant period in her life. So, she prayed constantly and found joy by meditating on several verses:

a. "If the unbeliever departs, let him depart; a brother or sister is not under bondage in such cases. But God has called us to peace. For how do you know, O wife, whether you will save your husband? Or how do you know, O man, whether you will save your wife? But as God has distributed to each one, as the Lord has called each one, so let him walk." (1 Corinthians 7: 15 – 17)

b. "All things work together for the good of those who love God who are called according to His purpose." (Romans 8:28)

c. "My God shall supply all your needs according to His riches in Christ Jesus." (Philippians 4: 19)

d. "Trust in the lord with all your heart, and lean not on your own understanding. In all your ways, acknowledge Him, and He shall direct your paths." (Proverbs 3:3-5)

e. "Many are the afflictions of the righteous: but the Lord delivers him out of them all." (Psalm 34:19)

Summary: Although she had some initial feelings of failure and concerns about how she would manage financially, Kelly's reliance on God's word rather than Satan's lies continues to sustain her and give her peace and joy.

Suzy Brown was divorced in 2000 after 33 years of marriage. "I was devastated on so many levels, I can't even describe them all," she said. "I was sick at heart about it, and I thought my life would be a sad, weak half-life until I died. But God has used this experience to bring me close to him in a way I never thought possible. This struggle has brought rewards I could never have imagined." Suzy founded the Midlife Divorce Recovery Group, whose mission is help women get through this unexpected life challenge and to create a life that's awesome. Through the group, hundreds of R.A.D.I.C.A.L. Women (Women – Rising Above Divorce In Confidence And Love) have found what they need.

8. Draw inspiration from how God brought you through a previous problem.

"Remember how the LORD your God led you all the way in the wilderness these forty years, to humble and test you in order to know what was in your heart, whether or not you would keep his commands. He humbled you, causing you to hunger and then feeding you with manna, which neither you nor your ancestors had known, to teach you that man does not live on bread alone but on every word that comes from the mouth of the LORD. Your clothes did not wear out and your feet did not swell during these forty years." (Deuteronomy 8:2-4)

a. List a problem that you had in the past.

b. Describe how God brought you through it.

9. Guard against negative statements/questions.

"We demolish arguments and every pretension that sets itself up against the knowledge of God, and we take captive every thought to make it obedient to Christ." (2 Corinthians 10:5)

Since you have grown accustomed to making negative statements/questions to yourself about your divorce status, you will be inclined to continue doing so. When you are tempted, ask yourself, "Is this statement/question aligned with what God says?" If not, immediately replace it with a verse from today's passage in Step 3.

Group Discussion - Living a Joyful Life

1. Define "Rejoice" in your own words.

_____

_____

2. Identify a problem you are facing or have faced in the past year.

_____

_____

3. Identify negative statements/questions you have said to yourself regarding the problem.

_____

_____

4. Identify at least one Bible verse that has helped you rejoice in the midst of the problem.

_____

_____

5. How do you think and act since you replaced negative statements/questions with a Bible verse?

_____

_____

Acknowledgments

Few readers rush to read the acknowledgments. However, for the author, it is an opportunity to express appreciation to some important people. My deepest gratitude goes out to the following people:

Hans Meeder, for encouraging me to write the book and offering suggestions for content.

Lynne Karanfil, for encouraging me to write the book, offering suggestions on content and format, proofread the manuscript and serving as a sounding board.

Pastor Timothy Siemens, for offering topics for inclusion and format, introducing me to counselors to get additional ideas for topics, and proofreading portions of the manuscript.

Pastor Mark Norman, for proofreading the manuscript and providing an endorsement.

Vernell Wheeler, for proofreading the manuscript.

Karen Gantt, for proofreading portions of the manuscript.

Richard McCray, for helping select the title, proofreading the manuscript and providing an endorsement.

Pastor Michael Moore, for proofreading a portion of the manuscript.

Carey Casey, for proofreading the manuscript and providing an endorsement.

Patrice Marshall, for providing topics for inclusion in the book.

Marja Humphrey, for providing topics for inclusion in the book.

Dedication

This book is dedicated to my late parents, Viana and Louis Williams. They stressed the importance of - and worked tirelessly to make sure all of their children had opportunities to receive – a quality education. This book is also dedicated to my siblings: the late Annie Williams Matthews, Bobbie Williams, Lena Williams Flaherty, the late James Williams, the late Nathaniel Williams and Lester Williams, all of whom seized the opportunity to go to school, thus setting tremendous examples for me to follow.

CPSIA information can be obtained
at www.ICGtesting.com
Printed in the USA
BVHW08s0721121018
529910BV00001B/192/P